WIFE, MOTHER, SPY

AN EXTRAORDINARY LIFE
FILLED WITH ORDINARY DAYS

ANN E. BUTLER

Print ISBN: 979-8-9912933-0-3

Ebook ISBN: 979-8-9912933-1-0

Library of Congress Control Number: 2024924818

Cover design by Ebook Launch

Printed in the United States

To my children – Claire, Kyle, Eric, Alexis and Katrina, for whom this story is written

And to Joe, who supported me unconditionally throughout my journey

While the experiences described in this book are all true, some of the names and many of the locations have been changed or obfuscated to protect national security secrets.

Contents

Introduction

Many women are mothers. Some mothers have five children. Some mothers have five children and work full-time. Very few mothers of five children work clandestinely as Central Intelligence Agency operations officers, spending countless hours in unpredictable and often dangerous environments with their families overseas. This I know to be true. This is my story.

It is a story about the intersection of marriage and parenting with a unique and challenging career. It is a look at my life and how I navigated the joys and heartaches, the thrills and letdowns, and the constant demands of being a wife, a mother to my five children, and a CIA spy.

Marriage can be hard. How do two people, previously strangers, fall in love and become permanent partners? How do they share everything—ideas, aspirations, emotions, money, and, perhaps most importantly, the critical task of raising children?

Parenting can be hard. How do two people, previously relatively independent, become responsible for other human beings—for their physical, mental, and spiritual growth?

Work can be hard. Now, add into the mix the difficult element of a career as an operations officer with the CIA. How does one person, previously carefree and on her own, balance the responsibilities of marriage, five children, and a job where she has to pick up and move not only herself but her entire family halfway across the world over and over? Especially with a job that requires always being "on," always paying attention to what is around you or who is near you, and always staying focused and aware of potential problems or threats.

This is the work environment I lived in every minute I was overseas—at the grocery store, at my children's school, or at a restaurant with my husband. It meant understanding that the mission comes first. It meant not being able to talk to friends and neighbors or even my husband and kids about what I did all day, every day.

Our entire routine was uprooted every few years. We had to relocate, not across town, not to a nearby city or another state, but from one country to another, crossing oceans and continents. We changed houses and schools. We said goodbye to friends and sought out new ones.

I had a critical, exciting, important career. It was, in fact, extraordinary. It required paying attention to every detail, no matter the hour of the day or night. I had to stay focused on the job and remain focused at home. I was responsible for people's lives at work and responsible for my family everywhere else.

I continuously questioned myself. How could this life be possible? Was I going to fail? Would I let someone down? Was something going to go terribly wrong? Would I put someone's life at risk? Would I miss a critical meeting with someone on a street corner? Would I forget to pick up one of my children? Would I be able to keep everything under control? How would I remember everything? *What was I thinking?*

To outsiders, I hoped I looked like any other working mom—going to the office, helping the kids head off to school, attending weekend outings, doing grocery store runs, watching kids' music performances, cheering at sporting events, and participating at neighborhood gatherings. I was undercover, so it was critical to look "ordinary." How was I able to successfully pull it all off? How did I maintain a "normal" family life and work this demanding, clandestine, 24/7 job?

Many nights I fell into bed exhausted, yet my mind still reeling, wondering whether I had missed something during the day, and reviewing and checking what I had to do next. I couldn't discuss my job with my friends, neighbors, or family members. I couldn't even join in a general conversation with them about my workday or whether or not I liked what I did for a living. Even a casual conversation ended up being too complicated because they would inevitably ask questions I couldn't answer.

I hope my story proves to all women—especially young women embarking on their professional lives who truly "want to have it all"— that an exciting, purpose-filled career *and* a family, however big that career and/or family may be, *is* possible. I want both women *and* men to know that it is possible to be both a good parent *and* a good CIA officer. It takes focus, discipline, and sacrifice—a lot of sacrifice. It demands *all* of one's time and effort. It requires plowing ahead even when things feel like they are falling behind…or falling apart.

Prologue

I was nine months pregnant with my second child when my two worlds completely collided.

It was early 1996, my 10th year on the job in the CIA. My husband, Joe, three-year-old daughter, Claire, and I were back in America, living in a comfortable, suburban neighborhood following an exciting and stimulating, albeit unexpectedly brief, year in Paris. We were settling into our new lives while eagerly awaiting my next assignment overseas.

Joe and I decided to name our second child, a baby boy, Kyle Joseph. He was due March 2nd. At my weekly prenatal appointment on February 20th, Dr. Seeker said there was a 70 percent chance that Kyle would be born before my next appointment, scheduled a week later, on February 27th.

Planning ahead, I decided to make my last day of work February 23rd. I felt good. I had things to do. There were cases to turn over, meetings to finalize, and reports to write. I needed the time to put everything together so I could relax and really focus on Kyle during my maternity leave.

It was Thursday, February 22nd. My office hosted a small surprise baby shower for me that afternoon. After enjoying the festivities for an hour or so, opening a few gifts and enjoying a delicious piece of chocolate cake with thick, blue, buttercream frosting, I dashed off. I had to pick up a colleague at the airport who was coming in from another city to collaborate with me on one of my cases. I had never met him in person, but I had a whole list of objectives to discuss with him that evening. It was an important case. The CIA wanted to maintain a relationship with a particular individual, Lawrence, our "asset." We believed that he had valuable information on the economic espionage efforts of foreign firms in the region, information specifically requested by US policymakers. We just had to convince Lawrence to tell us what he knew and, more importantly, use his access to find out more.

I drove one of the office cars to the airport. My plan was to pick up my colleague—a young officer named Tom—and then drive to a nearby restaurant for a brief dinner meeting to discuss the next day's agenda. Afterward, I would drop him off at his hotel, return the car to the office, and drive my own car back home. I had arranged the airport meeting via our secure communication method at the office.

Tom and I had already discussed how we would set up and conduct the meeting with Lawrence. It was going to be held in a relaxed venue and would give Tom a chance to explain to our asset the kind of information we were seeking, the reason it was so important, and set the stage for a follow-up meeting. Tom would then take over the case while I was away from the office on my maternity leave. We both knew and understood the plan. I had the restaurant picked out and the logistics under control. It was all so straightforward and simple.

I drove into the parking lot at the small, regional airport on the outskirts of town. Taking the ticket out of the machine, I continued through the gate and found a spot just a few rows away from the entrance.

With a slight bit of difficulty, given my large, nine-month pregnancy belly, I extricated myself from behind the wheel of the car. I was running a few minutes behind schedule. I don't like to be late for meetings, so I began to walk rather briskly toward the front door of the terminal. Suddenly, just before reaching the airport entrance, I felt a warm liquid running down my leg. Within seconds, my lower extremities were soaked. My water had broken, and Kyle was on his way! Thankfully, my dark navy blue, maternity pantsuit made the mess slightly less obvious.

I only had the office phone with me—a bulky, Motorola, antiquated-looking flip phone with a three-inch long antenna. But at least I could call for some help. I tried to reach my husband. *No answer*! I dialed again. Still nothing.

Next, I dialed our friend and neighbor, Virginia, whom we had arranged to watch Claire at a moment's notice. Then I called my doctor and, finally, my boss.

No one answered my calls. Had they forgotten that Kyle's birth was imminent?

Later I learned that the very day Claire's baby brother, Kyle, was about to enter the world, Claire and Joe had decided to head outside to an open field down the street from our home and fly kites. While I was filled with trepidation about how to handle the moment, they were going about their day entirely unfazed.

I proceeded with Plan A and met my colleague at the gate but quickly told him there was a slight change in the agenda, and a Plan B was urgently required. Tom was a fellow officer and understood the need to be flexible. We hurriedly walked back to my car, though it was becoming increasingly difficult for me, and my mind was racing. By this time, it was late afternoon, and many flights were arriving. My heart sank, and I began to panic as I saw the long line of cars snaking their way through the parking lot, all trying to exit at the same time.

We eventually joined the line, and losing my patience, I leaned out my window and shouted from the car, "I'm in labor and need to get to the hospital, please!" Miraculously, a few cars let me in front of them, albeit reluctantly, and I eventually inched ahead enough to get out of the parking lot. I wanted to yell to the cars behind me that I wasn't exaggerating and I really *was* in labor. But just then, I winced as I felt the contractions start.

Despite the hassle of being in labor and the quick change the trajectory of the day was taking, my colleague and I were both quite calm. After all, we were taught how to remain composed under crisis. I decided to drive since Tom was new to the area and didn't know the streets. It was not the way I had meticulously planned out the events of the day, but here we were.

Driving north, the doctor on call finally got back to me and told me to make my way to the hospital. What a novel idea. *No help there,* I thought sarcastically.

Realizing my office was about twenty minutes north between the airport and the hospital and that I might need some help, I called the office number again, and this time, I reached my boss, Kevin.

I had only worked for Kevin for about five months. He was a kind, personable, family man in his early fifties. He could be counted upon when needed. He was also committed to his work as an officer of the CIA, and although his day-to-day work wasn't as dangerous as our work overseas, he took his responsibility as head of the office seriously.

I wheeled into the office building's parking lot probably a little too fast. Kevin was waiting for us outside the entrance. He came to my side of the car, opened the door, and, without hesitation, told me to move to the back seat of the car and lie down. In his calm and confident manner, he immediately took over the driving. After making several wrong turns, the car bouncing over back roads, and me laughing hysterically each time my boss or my colleague cracked a joke about the whole affair—all of which exacerbated my contractions, which were now coming quite regularly—we arrived at the hospital.

The back seat of the car was soaked, but I had safely arrived at the hospital with two men, neither of whom was my husband…or the baby's father!

All ended well, of course. Joe eventually arrived. Kyle was born early the next morning. He was perfect. It was only later that day when I was sitting in the quiet hospital room with my newborn baby next to me that the realization sunk in. Despite all my efforts to plan for every eventuality, there would always be some things in this crazy life of mine (some very important things) that simply couldn't be planned.

CHAPTER ONE

BEGINNINGS

New York
1970-1985

Growing up with our parents in Upstate New York in our small, neat, white house on a street that dead-ended into expansive woods, my three brothers and I lived a simple, idyllic life.

Our wraparound deck looked out over a sprawling backyard with a big forsythia bush along one side that bloomed with sunny yellow flowers every year and two eight-foot-tall, fragrant lilac bushes along the other. A stone-terraced garden contained a huge array of peonies that came back every year with vibrant splashes of pink. In the middle of the yard, standing tall, was a dogwood tree that became a symbol and a sentimental point of remembrance of our formative years there.

My brothers and I walked to school, ran with friends in the woods behind the neighborhood, explored down by the river, played kickball in the corner lot around the block, joined our high school sports teams, and attended Friday night football games in our high school stadium overlooking the Susquehanna River.

The six of us ate dinner together every night around our small dining room table, which, as we all got older and bigger, became more crowded and more animated.

My dad's position as professor of geography at the State University of New York (SUNY) at Binghamton, where he ultimately became chairman of the department, meant he was naturally drawn to worldwide economic and political issues. He traveled quite a bit, often to exotic places, to attend conferences or conduct research.

I remember hearing stories of when he, with my mom and two older brothers in tow, traveled to Chile for six months to conduct field research for his dissertation—first in Santiago, then Concepcion in the southern part of the country. Before Chile, my dad had traveled to Ecuador, Peru, and Bolivia to conduct preliminary research for the textbook he was writing. He told us kids about his trip to Moscow when Russia was still firmly behind the Iron Curtain and his many trips to Mexico City and the Yucatán Peninsula to gain still more knowledge in his field of water resources.

Looking back, my father's excitement about the world was clearly the impetus for my desire to travel and experience foreign lands. My father was smart. Life excited him, and he always took advantage of opportunities to explore and grow in his field. He traveled with ease, threw himself into his research, and was a great teacher to his university students. He was well-liked and respected by them. He was also kind, generous, and dedicated to his family. For these and many other reasons, my dad is one of my greatest heroes.

On three separate occasions during his career, my father took each of my two older brothers and then me along with him during his excursions to Yucatán. These weren't the typical vacation getaways where you relax and soak up the sun all day. My dad was working. We were there alongside him, watching as he analyzed and compared water samples, discussed the results with his university colleague, walked the long, dusty paths to inspect dormant wells, and experienced firsthand the Mayan culture of the region.

In May 1973, it was my turn to travel with my dad. I was twelve years old. Together with his very good friend and longtime colleague, Professor Doehring, and Isolde, a graduate assistant in her fifth year of study, we spent a month traveling throughout Yucatán. We landed in Cozumel, where we spent the first couple of nights. We then ferried to Playa Del Carmen and boarded a crowded, hot, loud overland bus to Peto, a tiny town in central Yucatán. My dad had established close friendships with the Maryknoll missionaries, whom we fondly referred to as the "Padres," in Merida, Yucatán's capital. We traveled from one tiny village to another via Father Walter's Volkswagen van, stopping along the way to sample well water, collect critical meteorological data, and conduct "pump down tests."

Throughout the month, we experienced grimy hotel rooms, oppressive heat, humidity, ugly-looking insects, countless scorpions, iguanas, snakes, and, of course, Montezuma's revenge, a particularly potent case of diarrhea. We also enjoyed many meals and lots of social time with the Padres, saw a few secret Mayan ceremonies, climbed pyramids, ate lots and lots of fresh mangoes and papayas, and felt the tropical winds and Mexican sun as we dashed around on rented motor scooters. We traveled from village to village, passing quarries and wells in Punta Norte, Carrillo Puerto, and Merida, always coming back to our home base of Peto and the Casa Cural of the Padres.

It was a real adventure for me. I envisioned right then and there that this was the kind of life I wanted to live. I wanted to explore the world, but more importantly, I wanted to really feel the experiences in my core. Not just tangentially but deep down in my soul. And I wanted to explore the world with people I loved—family and cherished friends.

I often wish now I could have seen into my mom's and dad's thoughts as they were parenting me and my brothers. As I entered adulthood, became a wife, and then a mother, I realized that both of my parents had their own struggles, yet consistently put them aside to take care of us.

My father exhibited such selfless kindness to those around him and such incredible patience—with my mom, with us kids, with his parents, with his students, and with his colleagues. During a particularly difficult time in the 1970s when financial resources at SUNY Binghamton were becoming scarce, he dedicated months to the Department of Geography to ensure it stayed intact when it was in danger of being eliminated due to the budget cuts across the university. He wrote letters to the university leadership and met with countless senior administrators, endlessly advocating for his faculty and his students.

Separately, I saw how my father was a committed family man. After he passed away, I found hundreds of letters he had written to his parents. He had left home in 1943, at the age of seventeen, to attend the V12 Navy College Training Program at Cornell University. Despite the pressure of his studies in preparation to go to war, he took time every week to stay in touch with his parents. The V12 program was designed to supplement the force of commissioned officers in the US Navy during WWII. My father didn't hesitate to serve.

Throughout his life, I saw my father's dedication and love for his parents exhibited every time he was with them or talked about them. My father was a brilliant man and had incredible integrity.

My mom, too, was selfless. She always sacrificed for us kids. She took us shopping for a new set of school clothes every year but never bought herself anything new. She waited to ensure that everyone—including my insatiable, athletic brothers—had all they wanted to eat, and more, at dinner before she helped herself.

During our usual Sunday dinners of juicy, perfectly cooked roast beef, fluffy mashed potatoes, and steamed green peas, Mom always took less of everything so everyone else had full plates. She cooked, kept house, mowed the lawn, followed our school progress, and chauffeured us here and there. Then, because she wanted to make sure we would always be taken care of if anything ever happened to Dad, she went back to school and became a registered nurse at the age of forty-five.

After graduating with honors with her nursing degree, Mom worked the night shift, 11 p.m. to 7 a.m., just so she could be home to see us off to school *and* be there when we returned. My mom had her demons, though. She had a tough childhood and struggled with alcohol addiction her whole adult life. Yet, she always sacrificed her own happiness so we children felt happy, loved, and had everything we needed.

Mom paid a price for her sacrifices, though. She died young from a fall down a set of stairs under the influence of alcohol. She was only fifty-five. I was young, too. I had just turned twenty-four, far too young to lose my mom.

My mom's funeral was a blur. We couldn't process what was happening. My brothers and I all handled the death of our mom differently, each in our own way. She had been the rock of our family. None of us ever imagined she would be gone one day. None of us, including my father, really knew what to do next. Mom always knew what needed to be done and when. She knew how to take care of us. She was always there.

Recalling her death is still very painful. My heartbreak resurfaces every time I recall how lonely I felt when she wasn't there to see me get married or to welcome any of my children into the world. Over the years, I often felt envious of friends whose mothers were still alive and able to share in their daughters' lives.

When I sit quietly and reflect on the relationship I had with my mother, I know that she absolutely shaped the person I became, just as much as my dad helped start me on my career path. I am nowhere near as selfless or as self-sacrificing as my parents were. Somewhere along the line, though, many of my mother's actions in her best moments as a mom became mine, and many of my ideals and life goals were fine-tuned because of my dad.

Growing up, I learned what it meant to be supported by family. We had the same kind of bond that I have worked so hard to nurture in my own family. Unfortunately, I also learned how to handle disappointments, as many do in their youth. I sometimes expected too much. My relationships with my parents and my brothers were, at times, laden with challenges. But there was always a fundamental spirit of support among us.

I also learned that nothing is forever on this earth. Throughout my life, there have been countless times—and there will be many more, I am sure—when I wished my mom was just a phone call away. I wish I could ask her what she would do so *I* would know what to do. I now have three daughters, and I know they understand how special, how eternal, and how important a mother-daughter bond can be.

One of my father's greatest wishes was that my brothers and I would stay close to one another—that we would always be there for each other. My father told us that if we all watched out for each other, he could be confident that we'd all be okay once he was gone. We have all worked hard to carry out his wish.

Twelve years exist between my oldest brother, Joe, and my youngest brother, James. John and I fall in between. My brothers and I still share each other's struggles and joys. We are all excited about the accomplishments of the nieces and nephews—the graduations, college acceptances, weddings, and future plans.

We lean on each other when we face illnesses or deaths. We have all experienced our respective tragedies and crises. Some have been far worse than others, like the death of my nephew, Patrick, at the age of fourteen in a car accident. My brother and sister-in-law struggled through this together. The rest of us tried to be there for them, but we were suffering as well and really could never understand what they, as Patrick's parents, were going through.

Over the years, my brothers and I have often reminisced about our youth. We are the only ones left who were there, who remember…

There was the time my oldest brother, Joe, was told to keep an eye on me but was distracted and I fell, causing a permanent gash on my cheek. Although it's faded, it remains a reminder of that fateful day when my brother was "supposed" to be watching over his little sister.

Looking back, our parents gave us lots of autonomy. I remember making many of my own decisions, especially about what I wanted to do on weekends or "free" days.

Often, I'd roam the neighborhood with friends or traipse through the woods down to the steep cliffs over-looking the Susquehanna River that meandered past our backyard. I'd be gone for hours. I remember being surprised later in life when I learned that my high school was just under the two-mile limit that would have justified a bus ride—and that was only one way! I confidently walked that route without a second thought.

Our favorite path from the end of the street into the woods led us by a perfectly placed landmark. A large fallen log was positioned to act as the optimal seesaw. My friends and I would run a quarter mile to the spot, then all jump on the log. I usually flipped off as my end went into the air and sent me tumbling onto the hard earth. I'd get back up, fight for my spot on the log again, or just keep running through the woods, looking for the next adventure.

Somehow, even with after-school activities and so much freedom, we always knew when to come home. We felt safe and had lots of neighbors to keep an eye on us, even if only from their kitchen windows. Perhaps it was this fun, carefree youth that led me to push my own children out the door to play, to run around and explore, and to trust that they'd be okay no matter where in the world we were.

CHAPTER TWO

BRANCHING OUT

Notre Dame, France, Belgium, New York
1978-1985

My trip to Yucatán with my father and his colleagues as a twelve-year-old stirred in me an inexplicable but passionate determination to see more of the world. In high school, I traveled abroad again—first to Paris, and later, just across the border to Quebec. These were supervised trips, with teachers never far from us. Nonetheless, my friends and I did manage to evade authority for a few hours here and there.

In Paris, we stayed a bit longer than planned in the crowded, smoke-filled café on the Champs Élysées. When we finally realized the time and left, we thought we were headed in the right direction but soon somehow found ourselves lost in the complicated and confusing layout of the Latin Quarter. After many minutes of indecision and arguing about which way to turn, we finally found a route back to the bus and our very impatient classmates, using the Quai along the Seine as our guide. Later that same week, in the massive Louvre Museum, we wandered down too many corridors and couldn't find our way out in time to meet our curfew, again causing a slight bit of irritation from our usually patient chaperones.

In my freshman year at the University of Notre Dame, I entered a rigorous, five-day-a-week preparatory course designed to equip us for our sophomore year when we would spend more than nine months in France, completely immersed in the French language, studying at L'Université Catholique de l'Ouest in Angers.

There were times during that freshman year, before Angers, when I really struggled with my decision to spend an entire year abroad. Was I willing to miss nine months of being on campus and all the social activities that took place at Notre Dame? What about the Irish festival, AnTostal, that took place on the quads every spring, or the Irish Wake at Alumni Hall, or the famous Bookstore Basketball event? Did I want to miss Notre Dame football and the pep rallies each week? Or all the friends I had just made?

A month before the end of my freshman year, I sat in the lobby of Stanford Hall, talking with two close friends about my hesitation to leave campus. Within seconds of expressing my reservations, both friends immediately and almost in unison assured me that I was making the right decision. They said my friends would still be there when I returned, I would make more friends in Angers, and it was an opportunity of a lifetime. They were, of course, right. Looking back, it was that year in Angers that clearly set the stage and prepared me for what would become an unparalleled career.

We were given lots of freedom that year in France to travel around the country and throughout Europe. We spent weekends with classmates and new friends. I spent many afternoons alone hunting down the perfect, warm, buttery croissant. Our only requirement was to be present for classes every morning and to make the most of the experience. We knew we could make that work.

I lived with a wonderful family—Monsieur and Madame Verron and their seven-year-old daughter, Linda. They also had four older children, all married and living on their own. Their tiny, well-kept home was on a narrow street about thirty minutes from campus. Linda and her parents taught me the real conversational, familial French that I would end up using throughout my career and beyond. They also taught me about living every day in a family setting, the French way, with friends and neighbors stopping by often for a glass of wine or piece of tarte.

They treated me like one of their own. They, too, loved to travel, and after I started my career and moved around the world, they visited me and my family at many of our overseas locations.

Years later, during my Paris assignment as a CIA officer, I returned to Angers with Joe and Claire, my firstborn. We sat with the Verrons in the same home I had lived in for a year so long ago—before marriage, children, or a job. I felt a sense of comfort as I witnessed the intersection of that foundational year of my college experience with the career I hadn't realized I had been preparing for my whole life.

My positive experiences in France that sophomore year spurred me to apply for an International Rotary Scholarship upon graduation from Notre Dame.

I didn't get my first choice of France or my second choice of Switzerland, but I did get a year of study at l'Université de l'Etat à Mons in Belgium. I was disappointed that I would not be returning to France. I was sure that France was the perfect place for me. In fact, I had rather expected to be assigned there. After all, it made so much sense. However, I wanted to be grateful for the opportunity I was getting, and after some self-reflection, somewhere in the recesses of my soul, I knew the year would be an adventure. I was ready.

Armed with memories of traveling with my dad to the rural corners of Yucatán, his stories about his traveling further abroad, and my own experiences in France, I headed to Belgium. I was entirely on my own, not sure if my language skills would be sufficient to get me through daily routines, let alone a master's program taught entirely in French.

With a bit of trepidation, I made my way from the Brussels airport via two different buses, eventually arriving at the dormitory where I was assigned to stay for a month. I was scheduled to attend a few weeks at the University of Brussels in an intense French program before starting my graduate classes in an International Affairs program in Mons, south of Brussels, close to the French border.

I looked around my tiny room, dropped off my bags, and quickly realized that for the first time in my life, no one was going to tell me what to do next—it was all up to me. I headed out of the dorm complex and started walking down a wide boulevard with a grassy median in the center in search of a bite to eat. After about ten minutes passing shuttered stores, gas stations, and empty parking lots, I stopped at a café that, at a glance, looked comfortable enough. I headed to an empty spot at the bar, sat down on a high stool at the end, and ordered a classic Belgian meal of wine-soaked mussels and a strong, dark glass of beer. The conversation was all in French, of course. I remember thinking, *This is it. If I'm going to make this work, I better just throw myself in, full speed ahead.* Thankfully, my French didn't fail me. I settled in for the next hour to watch the comings and goings of the café patrons. Slowly, I began to feel like maybe, at that very moment, I belonged right there.

Back then, in the mid-1980s, communication to the US from abroad was expensive and inconvenient. Every three to four weeks once I started classes, I walked from my dorm room down the hill to the corner phone booth outside the university's main entrance. It took a lot of coins and a lot of patience, but I was eventually connected to my parents across the Atlantic. It was one of the few times each month that I spoke English, and then I only spoke it for about fifteen minutes!

Being entirely on my own, making new friends, learning my way around a new town, taking graduate-level classes, and writing my thesis—all in French—could have been overwhelming. However, there was something about making it on my own in a foreign country that I found exhilarating. Unbeknownst to me at the time, this was all part of the plan leading me to my ideal career.

After completing my Master's in International Trade and returning to America, I spent hours looking for that once-in-a-lifetime, perfect international career opportunity. I mailed out resume after resume and cover letter after cover letter. I applied to international banks, nonprofit organizations with projects overseas, multinational Fortune 500 companies, government agencies with an overseas nexus, and anything else that appeared to have that international flavor I was seeking.

And one option on that endless list was the Central Intelligence Agency.

Applying to the premier intelligence agency in the world was a long and arduous process—at least it was back in the mid-1980s. It involved filling out a thirty-page typewritten application, sending it in via the US postal system, then waiting…and waiting. This was followed by long periods of more waiting between phone calls. The calls never really provided any indication of my status in the application process or any information regarding the position I was seeking.

As I waited, I tried to stop wondering if and when I might cross the next step. I had come home after a substantively rewarding year in Mons ready to start my life somewhere in the big world. Yet here I was after graduation, still living in the same house in the same small, Upstate New York town in which I had grown up. I had aspirations. I wanted to do something exciting. I wanted, more than anything, to go back and live in France. Instead, as I waited and hoped for the career of my dreams, I worked two part-time jobs—one as a substitute teacher at the high school I had attended only a few years before and the second as a salesclerk at a local Radio Shack.

I enjoyed living with my dad again. We had always understood each other. He knew I wanted more for my career and life than to work as a substitute teacher by day and a salesperson behind a counter by night.

The high school teaching job wasn't so bad. I was a long-term French substitute and was teaching French alongside the same teachers who had taught me. It was comfortable and at least gave me a small window into life overseas.

However, I was still anxious about my future. It was expected that after four years of college, the start of a career would come next. But…in the Radio Shack in the only shopping mall in my hometown on Halloween night, a man I had never laid eyes upon, Joe Potak, and two good friends of mine walked in and changed my life forever.

I learned later that the evening was prearranged. Our friends, who were already a couple, had wanted us to meet, and they had already told Joe all about me. Sharon was my high school friend, and her boyfriend, Tace, was Joe's friend from kindergarten.

I had just served the last few customers of the evening and was ringing up the sale at the cash register. I was getting ready to close up the store and start vacuuming when I looked up to see the three of them—Sharon, Tace, and a tall, handsome guy—walk across the entrance threshold.

The stranger had dark, scruffy hair, a Fu Manchu mustache, and a twinkle in his deep, dark-brown eyes. He was dressed in a sailor uniform and carried a small American flag. I assumed it was his last-minute idea of a Halloween costume, and I stifled a chuckle. There was something intriguing about this stranger. I wanted to learn more.

When he came into the store again a week later, he was alone and dressed in normal street clothes. Again, he came in at the end of my shift. I was serving the last customers and planning to quickly close the store so I could head home. He waited. He seemed to be browsing the array of adapter cords, but as soon as the last customer left, he approached me and, with no preamble, asked me out for a drink. That evening, as we walked out of the Radio Shack, I could never have imagined the adventures we would ultimately experience together over the next several decades.

On that very first date with Joe, I made it abundantly clear that I wouldn't be around very long. I was moving on, I said. I'd be working and living abroad soon. I had dreams, plans, and goals. I had places to visit and countries to explore. He listened, probably not entirely understanding where this pent-up desire and outpouring of plans was coming from. Joe had spent six years in the US Navy, so he knew about being outside our little town. Yet, he just listened to me go on and on. Then, before the evening ended, he asked me on a second date.

Like Joe, I had lived in the Triple Cities, a small enclave of three southern New York towns across the border from Pennsylvania, almost my entire life. "But boy, oh boy, things are going to change," I told him.

CHAPTER THREE

FUNDAMENTALS

Virginia
1985-1994

I "entered on duty" with the CIA in April of 1986. By that time, I had been living at home for two years. I had finally received a response from the organization the previous autumn. They wanted to meet me. Unfortunately, the call came the month my mother died. I asked for a delay, certain that meant that I would lose my opportunity to work for the CIA, but of course, I had to take that chance. Instead, they expressed their condolences and scheduled a meeting with me in Washington, DC, two weeks later, in early November 1985.

I began in a classroom of new employees, all of us hoping to immediately begin the exciting career we were promised. We stayed together as a group for about a year during our introduction to the "Agency" and throughout initial training. We were all twenty-somethings and now surrounded by readymade friends. Except for being committed to work each day, we had very few responsibilities that first year. This made it easy for us to focus on our daily job of learning and honing our craft. I only had myself to worry about. I only had to work hard, learn the trade, and look ahead.

Training for this job was unlike the instruction required for any other job. I quickly discovered the distinctiveness of the training was indicative of the uniqueness of the career upon which I was embarking.

We learned about and practiced using different weapons—the 9mm Browning semiautomatic handgun, the 38mm Smith & Wesson revolver, shotguns, automatic rifles, and submachine guns. We learned how they worked, how to shoot them, when to shoot them, and how to take care of them so they would be ready when we needed them. We learned how to load ammunition and the differences between each type of bullet. We also learned about hand grenades. Since the US was still in the throes of the Cold War with the Soviet Union, we learned about Soviet small arms so we could understand the threat from the other side.

We underwent weeks of paramilitary exercises in the woods. We learned about the dangers and perils of night navigation. We learned survivability techniques, including escape and evasion.

Of course, on top of that, we also spent endless weeks learning how to be a spy, or rather how to recruit spies. We learned where to find them, how to talk to them, how to get them to commit treason, how to keep them and ourselves safe, and how to make sure we always had the upper hand.

We couldn't believe we were being trained for the ultimate clandestine career and getting paid at the same time! It soon became apparent that I would never be able to tell my children, my friends, or most of my family the realities of my job.

Lengthy training sessions in the woods were not geared toward teaching us how to survive in the elements for long periods of time. Rather, they were extreme enough to make us understand that we had to think quickly and carefully when we were away from shelter or the safety of our headquarters. We learned and practiced what to do and how to act when we were confronted with the unexpected. There were long days and nights where we had to forage for food and find our way out to a paved road using only a compass and our wits. In many ways, this strengthened our determination to succeed in this unique world of espionage into which we were stepping.

Over the years, in an effort to keep current with counterintelligence changes and world events, we regularly took classes about how to operate overseas, how to operate as technology evolved, how to stay substantively relevant, how to react quickly, and how to remain cognizant of changes on our playing field in order to stay on top of our game. We knew what we were learning and what we were doing was important. We could feel it. This constant and consistent training instilled in us a sense of confidence and of mission that we would carry through the rest of our careers.

Like all operations officers, I first learned my trade at our training site in Virginia. We sat in classrooms listening to seasoned case officers tell of their missions overseas recruiting agents and stealing secrets. The instructors led us through exercises that presented a long series of continuous physical and mental challenges. As they intertwined their stories with the rules of the road for our work, it was evident they missed being at the pointy end of the spear and in the middle of the action. These instructors had seen so much and experienced such incredible satisfaction with their work. It was exciting to listen to them and imagine the adventures we all had before us.

During my first year of training, I had an instructor named Stu. He was the one who directly oversaw my progress through the eighteen weeks of "Farm" training. He was the one who was responsible for giving me unequivocal feedback. He was the one who would guide me to a successful finish or make the decision that I wasn't cut out for this profession.

Stu had spent his career in Asia. He was quiet, but I could tell he was always listening. He was the kind of mentor you knew you had to pay attention to, because every word he said was important.

Stu was the observer for an exercise I had with another instructor, Allen, who was playing the role of someone I had to convince to work for the CIA. The evening before the beginning of this particular exercise—a culmination of several weeks of preparation—Stu passed Allen the name of a local restaurant I had chosen for the meeting location.

The afternoon of the meeting, I sat in a quiet part of the restaurant, waiting.

"Hello," Allen said haltingly as he approached the table, glancing around.

"Please…sit." I gestured across the table.

I began working through my mental agenda, asking about his family, his recent vacation, and his plans for the next few months. Then, as he became more relaxed and more comfortable on the restaurant bench seat across from me, I slowly asked more sensitive questions.

"I understand you have additional information of interest," I suggested.

Allen started throwing up roadblocks. "I do have some things I am certain you will be pleased to know, but first, I'm also certain that you will have no problem increasing my monthly pay by ten thousand dollars?"

I had to maintain control of the conversation. I knew this was make-believe, but even so, my next steps could end my training and the great plans I had for my future.

I thanked Allen for all he had done for us in the past, adding, "I very much appreciate your time and your ideas." Then, I spent quite a bit of time highlighting all the reasons why he was "picked" to work with us in the first place and why he was so incredibly valuable, all to play to his ego.

I also knew I had to address his request for ten thousand dollars, or he'd counter that I wasn't listening to everything he had said.

"Allen," I began, "you have worked with us a long time. You know that we have to confirm the information and justify the transaction. You know you can trust me. I believe your information is accurate, but I need to confirm it with my superiors."

Then Allen seemed to change course a bit. As if to test my knowledge of world events, he started to talk about what he knew with regard to the semiconductor industry and Asia's concentration in the market. He began to recount details of meetings he had participated in with senior executives of Japanese companies and their plans to saturate the market. Allen continued to challenge me, citing countries and their leaders as well as numbers, as if to throw me off my game.

He did his job. Once Allen, in his role as an agent, confirmed that I was knowledgeable of the issues at stake, he waited for me to counter his rebuttals and handle his request for payment. He asked how long he had to wait to get paid, if he was at risk, and how I would help him if he was caught talking to me. The back and forth with Allen was very realistic. I had to practice my responses, come up with answers on the spot, remain calm, and stay in control. Eventually, this pretend meeting ended amicably and, thankfully, successfully.

These carefully constructed exercises and the invaluable feedback afterward were designed to prepare us for the unexpected twists and turns we would certainly encounter once out in the real world.

During the eighteen-weeks of training, my entire focus was the job. I returned home to Northern Virginia a few times per month for only a day or two each time to catch up on sleep and recharge—then I drove back to the 24/7 schedule of training.

Suddenly, those brief stints at home, when I did such simple things like fill my car up with gas, stock my fridge with a weekend's worth of food, or do anything in the "real world," gave me a whole new appreciation of my work during those weeks in training. I realized I had undertaken something very different than what I saw happening on the streets every day. I understood better the risks I would be taking. I watched the news with a different outlook. I started closely following current events and wanted to learn more about the countries that the US interacted with on an economic and political level. To practice my newly acquired observation skills, I watched the people around me.

There were long, intense hours of repetitive instruction. On the range, I fired magazine after magazine of ammo from a Glock pistol, then moved to the next station, picked up an M4 long gun, and fired it over and over. Each time, I tried to get more exact with my aim and hit the center of mass.

Later, when exercises transformed into scenarios mimicking real life, we had to enter a building full of people shouting, explosions rocking the walls, and lights flickering on and off, and decide in an instant who were the "bad guys" that had to be taken down and who were the "friendlies." Though this was the time to make mistakes, each wrong decision, even in these practice scenarios, created uncertainty and a loss of confidence in myself—neither of which I could carry into the real world if I was going to make this career work.

During my first few years working in the CIA, I learned how to coordinate with many other US government intelligence agencies, the military, and agencies following domestic security issues. The CIA's role was often very different from that of the rest of the intelligence community. Long before 9/11 and the warzone activity that ensued, the CIA's mission addressed turmoil in many dangerous environments around the world. At those times, the CIA usually had to go it alone without the presence or assistance of the US military.

We had a different mission and a different way of achieving that mission. When time was of the essence, it seemed there was less bureaucracy to deal with in our organization. We were laser-focused on getting the job done, whatever it took. I realized this was how the CIA was different. Other agencies had important work to do too but when we were tasked with getting a piece of information or eliminating a threat or ensuring someone was extricated from a dangerous situation, we knew what needed to be done, and we were trained to do it quickly and with agility.

I was living in Northern Virginia. I spent long hours at the office reading about the important events of the day and thinking of ways we might be able to answer the policymakers' questions.

I attended many meetings downtown at the Federal Bureau of Investigation (FBI) headquarters on Pennsylvania Avenue in Washington with FBI agents who helped us analyze the domestic aspects of our operations overseas. I met with Army and Marine officers at the Pentagon to discuss how to incorporate their requirements into our operations. I attended National Security subcommittee meetings to ensure coordination among agencies regarding intelligence requirements and national security issues. Sometimes I sat in those meetings, back-benching and watching in awe as, right in front of me, decisions regarding how to protect our country were being made.

The people making these decisions were working long hours, not for themselves but for our country. It reinforced for me how important their work and even mine was to the people of the United States. It was a realization that I knew few people understood.

Overseas, I learned that the best ideas often came out of collaboration with fellow officers. Whether there were three, five, or ten people in an office, we bounced ideas off one another. We ran through our plan minute by minute, ensuring it all made sense. Is this a good spot to stop during my surveillance detection route (SDR)? How do I convince my agent to travel somewhere dangerous? What's a good, out-of-the-way place to meet? What else can I offer my agent?

Everyone in our office had experiences that could benefit the others. It always felt as though we were all on the same team. We hollered over the short cubicle walls. We sat around the conference table with sandwiches and sodas and discussed our cases—the highs and lows, the glitches, and the things that worked flawlessly.

Early in my career, I spent three weeks at a language school in Spa, Belgium, for a quick but intensive refresher course in French. I was lucky to already have foundational knowledge in the language from my high school and college years. The CIA stresses foreign languages for its officers. So much more information can be obtained from sources and stronger relationships can develop with people simply by speaking to them in their own language. I always learned the basics of the language where I was going. It paid enormous dividends.

Sometimes while working, I traveled under a different name to protect myself and the identity of those I was meeting. My first step was to leave via train or car to cross a border, then travel to another city via train or plane, eventually arriving at a prearranged location to meet my agent—all under my alias name.

I was fitted for several different disguises before my first assignment overseas. For our protection, we sometimes wore a "light disguise" when meeting someone we knew we would likely not see again, like a "walk-in" or someone who came to the embassy claiming to have information. It was something simple—a wig, facial marks, glasses—and always included a fake first name. My simple, quickly thrown-together disguise that I kept handy in the safe next to my desk consisted of a blue patterned scarf, a pair of brown-framed glasses, makeup a shade darker than my complexion, and a mole to place on my left cheek. It was easy to use, quick to pull together, and compact enough to keep in my purse if I needed it in the field. They were all common enough items that no one would question why I even had them. I could easily and quickly change my appearance and present myself differently to someone I would never see again.

The wig was slightly more complicated. It was something I wore when I had to dramatically change my appearance— such as having to get in and out of a place or to determine if someone was following me. It totally transformed my look.

I was a natural auburn with shoulder-length hair. The wig gave me a brown bob with bangs. It was a much stodgier look than I would have liked, especially when adorned with a drab-colored scarf and small pearl earrings. They were items I would never normally wear, which was, in fact, the point.

In our office overseas, we sometimes played a game that whoever pulled the shortest straw got the "opportunity" to meet with a walk-in. These "walk-ins" always thought the information they had was what everyone was waiting for. They knew they would get an audience at the embassy, even if just for a few minutes, and they wanted to take advantage of the opportunity to sell their information. Of course, we had our methods for corroborating the accuracy of any such information. There was an official protocol in place.

We went into these meetings with little hope of finding that golden nugget. It was rare to find the exact piece of information that would change how our country interacted with Russian leaders or the Iranian government. Nonetheless, every meeting was taken seriously. During the hostage crisis of the 1980s, when over a hundred foreigners were kidnapped in Lebanon by Hezbollah, a radical Shi'a Islamist organization, anyone suggesting they had information about the location of the hostages was listened to immediately. No officer wanted to be the one who let a bit of key information go unreported, especially when lives were at stake.

North Africa
1999-2000

It was a Wednesday in April 1999. I was married now, with three children: Claire, seven years old, Kyle, three and Eric, almost one. At the office, I was writing my reports from the agent meeting the night before and prepping for an official liaison meeting I had that afternoon across town with the local police. These meetings with the host law enforcement agencies and the local intelligence services were critical. They provided opportunities to share information and ideas in order to keep our host country secure as well as ensure US objectives were understood. Nonetheless, these interactions were just one of many facets of the job. So, as always, I had a list of tasks I had to accomplish and about four hours before I had to get dinner on the table for the kids at home and change clothes for a diplomatic reception happening later that evening. I was feeling good about my progress. I knew what I had ahead of me. Then, I drew the short straw.

The phone sitting on a desk in the middle of our office bullpen rang. It was the Marine guard at Post One, the entrance to the main Embassy building. He said there was someone at the front gate who wanted to talk to the CIA.

"I've got to finish this report," I quickly said to the others sitting in nearby cubicles.

John stood up and called out, "Leaving now. Have to start my SDR. Meeting is at eight tonight."

Sarah apologetically looked at me and explained she had a meeting with the chief beginning any minute.

I sighed and gathered my disguise kit and a pad of blank paper. Before heading out of the office, I called the Marine at Post One back to ask if this specific individual spoke English or even French. If so, I'd be able to make a quick determination of the validity of his information. The Marine told me, "He speaks a bit of English and seems to understand more, but his mother tongue is Dari."

I took a deep breath. I knew it would be a long meeting.

More often than not, individuals approaching an embassy like this would be slightly psychotic opportunists, simply there to tell a story of how there was a chip in his or her head or that they had the answer to the location of the holy grail if we would only pay a mere one million dollars.

For over two hours on this particularly beautiful spring afternoon, unfortunately, I was the only one available to listen to an elderly gentleman describe how he was convinced he was being followed by Russians.

"They've been after me for weeks," the tall, disheveled, shabbily dressed man whispered in a confident yet frightened tone. "I am sure they've tapped my phone. I feel my life is in danger."

"Why do you think you're of interest to the Russians?" I asked, revealing no emotion.

"I know their secrets regarding nuclear warheads that can be launched from space." The man cleared his throat, averting his eyes from mine.

It was at that point I knew it was all a hoax. My thoughts were confirmed when I asked the gentleman what exactly he wanted.

"I need protection and a hundred thousand dollars. In exchange, I'll give you proof that everything I'm saying is true."

I gently but firmly thanked him and told him we'd be in touch if necessary.

"How will you know how to reach me?" He squinted his eyes.

"We'll find you if we need to." I shook his hand. Of course, he believed we could find him wherever he was. We were the CIA.

Every meeting needed to be documented, even a meeting with someone we knew had no information of interest and were certain we would never see again. If this person ever entered another embassy, as long as our history with him was documented, it would be only minutes before we'd realize he was just shopping his "secrets" around.

Just a few years into my career, my training and preparation were put to the real test. Everything was carefully arranged beforehand, including the exact place and time to meet as well as the introductions and actions that would indicate I was meeting the correct person. There were no cell phones, so there was no way to double-check or confirm I was in the right place. I just had to get to the prearranged location at the precise time. Sometimes, it was an expansive park with numerous ways in and out or a path along a creek near a neighborhood. Sometimes, it was an out-of-the-way corner near a busy shopping area.

On this day, exactly at noon, I entered a large city park via a prearranged northern route. I knew I had to arrive at 12:15 p.m. at a particular statue exactly 252 meters along a dirt path that wound around a lake. I also knew a colleague from the local office was expected to enter from the western side of the park and show up precisely ten minutes past the hour at the statue. I was confident the meeting would work. I was wearing my brunette wig, sunglasses, red lipstick, a royal blue scarf with a gray blazer, skirt and matching heels. My colleague and I had arranged all the details beforehand from our offices via our secure network system. That said, I always—every single time—held my breath, asking myself over and over if I had the correct information or if I had misread some key instruction as I casually strolled along the path, pretending I was simply on a lunch break from my job in the city.

I knew the backup plan if things fell apart. But I also knew that triggering the backup would cause a cascade of other critical problems. I certainly didn't want to be the cause of those.

The meeting was successful. As I arrived at the statue, my colleague came out of the shadows along a perpendicular path.

We both smiled and silently acknowledged one another. There was no time for high fives or chitchat. I slowly exhaled, took the envelope from my colleague and passed the package I had prepared for him. Within three or four seconds, I quietly slipped away via another path.

We had no GPS, no route checks via cell phone, and no way to call for directions. If there was an unforeseen circumstance or problem, I had to handle whatever obstacle was thrown my way. I needed to plan ahead for every detail and every minute of what I was about to do. I had to ensure there was a backup for every eventuality, and most importantly, I had to have the confidence to handle whatever circumstance might arise.

I wrote a lot of intelligence reports. We practiced this kind of writing over and over. In training, we were given all kinds of scenarios then told to pick out the important facts and put them into a format that would ultimately go into the intelligence reporting system, where it could then be disseminated to policymakers. There was a specific way to cite the information: the important facts came first, followed by obfuscating details about the sources and a detailed yet concise explanation of how they got the information in the first place. Did they work in the office that generated the information? Or had they heard about it in a meeting? Had they been given the details by someone else who worked in the office?

We learned how to sift through everything we heard and then ferret out the critical pieces. We learned to write succinctly without talking about ourselves or highlighting the questions we were asking. The report had to stand alone.

We also had to write truthfully. We honed our ability to write clearly and concisely. The policymakers reading our reports didn't have time for our personal opinions or what we thought might have happened. They had to make quick, powerful decisions and needed concrete, unfiltered facts.

I reported what I was told by the asset and what pertained to the specific questions I had asked the asset during a previous meeting. My report cited *exactly* what he or she said, *exactly* what the asset was concerned about, or in other words, the *exact* secrets they were passing to us. I never tried to interpret what they said. I listened carefully. If I could take notes, I did. If not, I tried to scribble enough afterwards so I could reconstruct the details back at the office. The ideal situation was sitting across from my agent in a well-lit room with hours to spare. That type of scenario, unfortunately, was rare. The report's importance was based *entirely* on the access the asset had to the information. That's what mattered. I was just the intermediary.

In each report, I included a separate section where I noted *my* thoughts, *my* assessment of the asset's access, and *my* understanding of why the asset was providing the information. I marked this part of the report as the "writer's assessment" so as not to confuse any of it with the facts from the agent.

I became good at calculating the moods of my assets, confirming they knew what they were doing and that they understood the risk of continuing to meet with me to provide secrets. I developed an ability to determine how well my assets could follow my directions or would be likely to follow them under stress. There were times when I had to make the decision to end our relationship with an agent. After lots of meetings and a lot of questions, I decided the agent could no longer be trusted, was focused on too many other things, had lost access, or was taking too many risks.

Najeem, an asset from a North African country, and I had been working together for almost two years. His information about changes in the regional political scene was satisfactory. It wasn't earth-shattering, but it was consistent. His knowledge of how people were getting in and out of the country we were monitoring was also somewhat useful. However, he started arriving late for meetings. He always made the alternate meeting time, but his reasons for missing the original time were weak, such as he had been talking with friends and lost track of time, or he had taken the wrong bus. I was losing confidence in his ability to take our meetings seriously. When he asked for a raise in his salary, I knew it was time to discuss my concerns about the change in his performance. I soon realized that Najeem couldn't get any additional information for me. He was just afraid to let me down. In the end, he was relieved not to have to pretend anymore. He understood the importance of telling the truth. I thanked Najeem for his time over the past two years, gave him a nice monetary bonus, and told him we would reach out in the future if we thought there was a role for him.

It was important to constantly evaluate our sources. It kept everyone honest.

Chapter Four

Life Partners

New York, Virginia
1984-1986

It was a cold, windy night in November. We met in the bar of a hotel downtown. The hotel had been there for years. It wasn't fancy, but it was easy to find, parking was simple, and the bar had a nice ambiance. I sat across from this handsome young man who had asked me out only a few days before. I wasn't interested in a relationship with anyone. I had other plans. But I told myself to just relax and enjoy the evening.

It was only a first date. I wasn't focused on anything past that evening. Rather, I was thinking about my future. I was always thinking about where I was going next, where I would work, what I would do, and where I would live. I was looking ahead. I had places to go and things to do. I was sure great things were ahead of me.

He made me laugh. I liked his company. We talked about traveling and all the places we had been. Joe had spent time in Japan and the Philippines when he was in the Navy. He had already seen a lot of the United States, much more than I had, in fact. He told stories of fun places he had traveled to and the friends he had made. He talked about his motorcycle adventures, recounting stories of people he had met as he rode back and forth across the country. It was a comfortable evening. Our conversation was effortless.

The hotel bar had a pleasant vibe. The popular tunes of the decade were playing in the background but not too loud. The music seemed to lower expectations as if to acknowledge that the place was just a meeting spot for old friends.

We weren't very far along into our evening before I made it clear to Joe, once again, that I didn't intend to stay in my hometown very long. I told him I had plans to move overseas—or at least I hoped to. Joe didn't react. I'm not sure what I was expecting, but even after my "big reveal," we just kept talking. To emphasize the point that it was just a fun get-together and nothing more, I insisted we go Dutch, and when the last call was announced, I proceeded to pay for my own drinks. Again, Joe seemed nonplussed. He seemed to just be enjoying the evening like I was—nothing more.

We weren't done talking and sharing stories, though. So, we drove, separately, to a nearby diner that was open twenty-four hours. In a red-vinyl, cushioned booth under bright, overhead lights that I worried showed every flaw on my face, we ordered milkshakes and kept talking.

I didn't leave town that week or that month. In fact, it would be another two years before I moved away from Upstate New York. In the meantime, Joe and I dated and met each other's families and friends. We traveled up and down the East Coast of the US, exploring together. We shared our hopes and plans. We celebrated holidays together. When my mom died unexpectedly, only a year after we started dating, I leaned on Joe tremendously. My father and brothers were grieving in their own way. I needed someone next to me, and fortunately, Joe was there.

Then I got the phone call I had been waiting for. An opportunity I couldn't refuse. I was offered a full-time position with the CIA. Finally, my dream job. Now, I could start my life—the life that I had been dreaming of, planning for, and working towards—and live and work overseas. I'd already had a few interviews with international banks in New York City, but this took precedence. This was the CIA! I knew I had to tell Joe what was going on.

By this time, Joe and I had been dating for about eighteen months. I told myself that everything I had done in my life so far had set me up for this moment—a job in Washington, DC, with the CIA. I couldn't give up my hopes and dreams. I had to go. I had to jump into this once-in-a-lifetime opportunity. So, I left New York and headed for DC.

Of course, I realized this would change the trajectory of my relationship with Joe dramatically. Though we had not talked seriously about a future together, I knew we were quite compatible and falling in love. It was fun just to be together. By that time, we had shared so many ups and downs. We both took the idea of a long-distance relationship in stride.

Joe helped me find an apartment in Northern Virginia, not too far from CIA headquarters. It was a cozy one-bedroom that was perfect for me. Then he helped me move everything in. It was eventually time to say goodbye. So we did with a sad but feeble promise to stay in touch.

I started my new and exciting career in the shadow of a city where great decisions were being made every day. I made friends among my new colleagues. We all had similar interests and goals. We were all striving to do something great in support of our country. I was busy learning my new trade, how to find my way around a new city, and how to navigate the halls of CIA headquarters.

Unbeknownst to me, while I was getting settled and comfortable in my new place, Joe was looking for a job in Northern Virginia. Then, one day, he told me he had found a position with an engineering firm and was going to move down to join me.

I was caught off guard. Was this what I really wanted? How would this new development change things? Would I be able to do it all?

Now in the same location, Joe and I dated another year. We eventually got engaged, and then six months later, we married. Our life together began simply—work, friends, getting our first puppy, buying our first house, buying a lawnmower, and trips back to New York to visit family.

In 1992, our first child, Claire Janet, was born. We settled into parenthood easily. It was seamless. Right away, Claire became part of our unit. We took long walks with Claire and our dog, Adrienne, up and down the cul-de-sacs and along the creek that bordered the neighborhood. It was a simple, uncomplicated, delightful life.

Something was simmering in me, though. I wanted to go back to Paris. My French was fluent enough and I wanted to use it. Life was good for me at that moment, but I wanted something more. Then, I was offered an assignment, an opportunity to make it all happen. Joe and I had settled into a comfortable routine. Now, I was threatening to turn everything on its head. Still, how exciting…we were going to be posted as a family overseas. It was a dream come true. I was assigned to the Embassy in Paris!

Together, we told family and friends, explaining only that I had a great opportunity to work overseas and we couldn't wait to start the adventure. More times than not, no one really understood, or maybe they just didn't want to hear it.

Neither of us was concerned about traveling across the ocean with a baby girl and a large dog. Our faith—in God and in each other—pushed us along, telling us the best way to see the world was right then and there.

Chapter Five

Starting in Paris

Paris
1994-1995

Our lives overseas began. My first assignment abroad, in Paris, began in June 1994. Joe, Claire, and I had spent a hectic last day at a Residence Inn hotel in Northern Virginia. We had moved out of our house and shipped everything we would need for the next three years to Paris. We had our plane tickets in hand. All that was left was to double-check that we had our passports and that our two-year-old had a change of clothes, diapers, and her beloved stuffed clown.

We asked a friend to ship one of our car seats when we found out at the last minute that we had too many carry-ons and suitcases. We ordered a taxi and headed to the airport.

When the cab pulled up and we opened the back passenger door to let Adrienne, our three-year-old black lab mix, hop onto the very worn, very cracked vinyl back seat, I thought the driver was going to have a heart attack.

"What the—" was all the taxi driver could blurt out, his worn, scarred face turning red and his bloodshot eyes bulging out of his head. The guy looked like he worked for Don

Corleone in *The Godfather* movies, and yet here he was, scared to death of our very mild-mannered, happy-go-lucky puppy. His hand actually clutched his chest.

"Calm down, sir," I said with exasperation as I maneuvered myself next to the dog and the car seat holding Claire. "She'll be fine. She's very gentle. No need to panic." Needless to say, in our stressed and somewhat emotional state getting ready for our first overseas family adventure, we had little sympathy for the taxi driver.

That ride to the airport turned out to be a sign that this trip would not go as smoothly as we hoped.

This was Adrienne's and Claire's first (of many) transatlantic flights. And, unfortunately, this first plane ride was a disaster. In addition to our dog and baby, we struggled to haul our seven suitcases and six carry-ons through the airport. Those bags held everything we would need for the next few months. I kept counting and recounting our bags, frantic that one would go missing. We stood in an interminable line, making our way through security, finally boarded the plane, then sat, delayed, on the runway for hours. Our 6:20 p.m. planned departure turned into a 9:45 p.m. actual take-off as we experienced the thunder and lightning become louder and scarier outside the plane's windows and wondered how Adrienne was faring in the cargo hold.

After a long, cramped flight, we arrived at Charles de Gaulle Airport in Paris, and the trip finally proceeded to run a bit more smoothly. All our bags arrived and, more importantly, Adrienne was fine. We were met at the airport by two of my colleagues, who we followed to a waiting van large enough for all of us and our luggage. By dinnertime, we were hunkered down in a comfortable, albeit a bit worn, apartment at the Boulogne compound. Located just outside the Paris city center, it's where we would stay for several weeks until our permanent place was ready.

For years, I had dreamed of living in Paris. I had always wanted to end up in the City of Lights. This was Joe's first time. The idea of the two of us together in Paris was monumental for me. I wasn't there for a quick weekend excursion or even a two-week vacation playing tourist. I was going to *live* here.

Once we got over the jetlag, we walked and explored and walked some more. Our car was still on a container ship somewhere over the Atlantic, so we explored the city on foot and tried to navigate the metro. On our very first day, we headed directly to the country's most famous landmark, the Eiffel Tower. We sat underneath the majestic steel arches with dozens of people around us speaking different languages. African merchants set up their wares in between the supports of the monument, selling toys that lit up and made noise and flew in all different directions. We looked up in awe through the mesh of intricately laid beams and just stared. Right there, we sat and ate our ice cream. At that moment, we didn't have a care in the world. It was probably then that we realized we really weren't tourists any longer—we were officially residents of Paris!

We sat in a Parisian café to people-watch and take in our surroundings. This activity quickly became one of our favorites in every country we lived in and visited. Sitting at a café at Place du General Gouraud down the street from our new home in the seventh arrondissement where Rue de l'Exposition, Avenue de la Bourdonnais, and Avenue Joseph Bouvard all join together, amidst the shoulder-to-shoulder tables and everyone smoking, was so…*Parisian*. No one was in a hurry to leave. No one, it seemed, had anything more important to do than sit there sipping a beverage and reading a newspaper.

We sat and watched people around us come and go. It was a perfect way to spend a morning, an afternoon, or an early evening. Relaxing in a café with a kir, my go-to French cocktail of white wine and cassis, was therapeutic. I decided right then that I could get very used to ordering a *café au lait* in the morning, an espresso in the afternoon, and a *vin blanc* or a *bière* in the early evening, all the while just sitting and pondering life.

I could feel the energy of the city around me. We could focus on our little three-person family and plan our next adventure for the week, or we could watch those near us and imagine their stories.

Now, years later, we still have our favorite Parisian spots, the ones with good views of interesting people, ornate buildings, or different perspectives of the skyline: Place de la Trocadero, where we had photos taken of all our kids over the years with the Eiffel Tower looming in the background, Rue Saint Dominique with its colorful fruits and vegetables on market day, or the Marché des Puces where we'd spend all day looking for that rare, cast-off treasure.

During our first time in Paris, we were only responsible for our baby girl and, of course, our dog. Adrienne needed to be walked regularly and had to become accustomed to apartment living. Before, she had always had the run of the house and a door that led directly outside to a grassy lawn. Now, she was forced to wait for us, take a tiny elevator to the ground floor, and stay on a leash. Such restrictions! But walking Adrienne gave us an opportunity to explore this incredible place even more. There were so many parks to discover and so many places to just sit and soak up the life of the city.

We walked by, through, and around the Arc de Triomphe, Place de la Trocadéro, Les Invalides, Pont Alexandre, the

Louvre, Sacre Coeur, Hotel de Ville, Pompidou Centre, Les Chatelet, Cimetière Père Lachaise, Musée du Vin, Bois de Boulogne, and more. Joe and Claire spent day after day exploring. I joined them whenever I could.

Up and down the long flights of stairs into and out of the metro we went, with Joe carrying the stroller. The Paris metro is extensive and reaches every corner of the city. It stops in every neighborhood and traverses every park, every bridge, and, it seems, every intersection. One could ride forever and circle the entire city, all for just a few francs. I always wondered, though, how people with any kind of mobility issues or anyone carrying more than one stroller could negotiate the underground labyrinth.

As he became used to the technique, Joe often lent a hand to other parents in the metro with a stroller in tow who were clearly trying to handle the ups and downs. He would spot the mom or dad standing at the top of the stairs of an underground entrance, peering into the darkness, trying to figure out how to manage.

It was a testament to Joe's insistence and interest in getting out to explore that he never let a child in a stroller— or later, five children—stop him. He took full advantage of our overseas adventures, determinedly seeing every hidden spot of every city and town. Invoking his mantra of never returning from somewhere by the same route, he stopped at every statue and every plaque, then found another one on the opposite side of the street. He learned every corner, every possible route in and out of places, and every landmark along the way.

I needed to learn the streets too, but for a very different reason. I was constantly looking for places to conduct my meetings. I looked for routes to and from these meeting places, selecting out-of-the-way, discreet restaurants or cafés. While we wandered around Paris as a family, in my mind, I filed away locations, landmarks, and quiet places to meet informants. There was never really a separation between my work and family life. When I was playing, exploring, or just walking the city with my family, I was also always working.

We'd meander together, Joe looking for the perfect resting spot and me looking for the perfect meeting spot.

I felt incredible pressure to succeed in my work. I didn't want to make mistakes. As one of the more junior officers in Paris, I knew my actions and decisions were being heavily scrutinized.

Nonetheless, it *was* Paris, and we wanted to enjoy its romance. Only a few weeks after we arrived, Joe and I celebrated our sixth wedding anniversary. We arranged a babysitter for Claire and spent the evening in the Latin Quarter, only a few metro stops from our apartment.

It was a balmy Saturday evening. The St. Germain de Près area in the sixth arrondissement was swarming with people. We walked across the bridge and found a cute little restaurant with tables spilling onto the pedestrian route. People were everywhere, restaurant hosts attempted to flag down prospective customers, and bands of musicians walked through the maze of streets. Though we were sitting at our little table only a few inches from the next, it seemed as though we were all alone. It was very romantic. How did we end up here? Two ordinary people, now living in Paris, celebrating an anniversary in a charming little hidden corner of the Latin Quarter before returning to their apartment in a grand, quintessential, nineteenth-century building overlooking the Champs de Mars and the Eiffel Tower. How *did* we get so lucky to end up here?

Over the next months, we became quite spoiled by this new life of ours. We'd find our favorite markets with the freshest food and discover bakeries where everything was made daily. The bread was so fresh it was as if the baguettes came out of the oven in our own kitchen. Each morning, on the way to Claire's preschool on Rue de Grenelle, we'd stop at the "Pink Boulangerie," a bakery painted bright pink on the outside with gleaming pink counters inside and the freshest croissants. The aroma of these freshly baked breakfast treats and soft loaves of bread was irresistible. After picking Claire up in the evenings, we stopped there again, this time to pick up two soft, warm baguettes—one for our dinner table and one for Adrienne to snack on as we continued our walk home.

There is nothing better than a warm, soft, fresh loaf of French bread and a hearty glass of red wine with dinner or a large, buttery croissant and a café au lait to start the day. We fully acclimated to those days in Paris. The feel, the smells, and the sounds of the city are rooted in our minds.

We bought Claire her first bicycle for 450 French francs from a store on Rue Jean Jaures in Boulogne. Joe had passed the store every day on his walks with Adrienne. He had spotted the bike weeks before and knew it was perfect. It had training wheels and a hand brake for the front tires. Its purchase—the first bike for our first child—was like crossing the threshold into life as parents. Claire stood next to her new bicycle on our balcony in Boulogne. She was only two but seemed twenty—confident and ready to take off and explore the world!

On a Sunday stroll to the Ile de la Cité, we mistakenly got off one metro stop earlier than planned and came up to the street level at Cluny Sorbonne. It was a fortuitous mistake. As we headed toward the Cathedral of Notre Dame, we passed the street where President Francois Mitterand had a well-guarded house. A prominent politician who served two terms in the 1980s and early 1990s as President of France, he was the first socialist to hold the office. He died six months after we left Paris, in January 1996, at the age of eighty.

All this exploring was terrific. I knew, though, I was there to work. While it was a privilege to be living in Paris, I realized I had to earn the privilege to stay.

Chapter Six

Moving Up

Paris
1994-1995

After ten days in Paris, our air freight arrived. Until then, life in the house was spartan, as it was at the beginning of every move. We made do with what we were able to fit into our suitcases and the few kitchen and linen supplies provided by the office (which never seemed to be sufficient as our family got bigger and bigger). So, this first air freight delivery felt a bit like Christmas. We were giddy pulling out our belongings one by one, things we had forgotten we even had, then finding the perfect place for everything in our new home. After we unpacked, the big, heavy-duty moving boxes made perfect little buildings for Claire's pretend forts.

Joe's computer and Claire's crib were two of the most important items we pulled out. The computer was so Joe could look for a job, and the crib was so Claire could sleep! Daylight hours were long, and Claire couldn't understand why anyone would go to bed when there was still plenty of light and playtime left on the clock. The time change was difficult for her and, as a result, for us. Joe and I sat outside her room night after night, listening to her sob and sob, pleading to be let out of her room so she could "play kitchen" with her plastic food and tiny pots and pans. How could we explain to her that going to sleep would be for her benefit? After what seemed an eternity, quiet finally enveloped the apartment. I'd soon begin to worry again, though, because it was too quiet. Nonetheless, I didn't dare crack the door of Claire's room as I knew that would just start the whole process all over again.

Those were frustrating times, and clearly cut into the magic of being in Paris. We all had to get used to falling asleep when it still seemed like daytime outside. I still had to get up early each morning to make my way to the Embassy, where I was learning a brand-new job. There was very little time to rest.

From the Boulogne compound, we moved to an apartment on Rue Elisée Reclus. It was in a grand, Haussmann-era building. Its cream-colored, stone façade overlooked the Champs de Mars park, which stretched out in front of the Eiffel Tower. The iconic landmark loomed outside the floor-to-ceiling windows of our living room.

Most of the tenants in this exquisite, historic building were older, very wealthy Parisians. Then, there was us. We were not the typical tenants of a seventh arrondissement apartment. Until we made a connection with the other residents, we regularly received the odd look from them. The owners of these high-end apartments clearly wondered how such an unexceptional, ordinary-looking American family could reside in such a luxurious place in such an extravagant corner of Paris.

Many times a day, we left our apartment on the third floor, took the tiny, mechanical elevator that we could barely fit into down to the ground level, and stepped into a palatial entranceway. Walking out two high oak doors and onto a wide sidewalk in front of the building, we turned southwest and walked one block to the Champs de Mars park where, under the shadow of the Eiffel Tower, we'd spend a very ordinary afternoon throwing a ball to Adrienne and pushing Claire on her little pink bicycle.

We walked along the Seine, following the river's path to the Ile de la Cité. We took walks in the rain when we couldn't even see the outline of the grand government buildings along the Quai, walks cutting through hidden alleys between the grand boulevards, and walks along the busy shopping street of Rue de Grenelle where Adrienne waited outside a market while we picked up groceries.

Entertaining was easy in our small but stunning apartment. We had a working marble fireplace in every room, and lots of natural light poured through the full-length windows into the sitting room and the dining room. The boulevard in front of the building was quiet and calm and lined with huge oak trees.

I worked hard to meld my responsibility for finding and ferreting out information of importance to our government with my day-to-day family activities. I had to make both work together. Finding people who had secrets and who would be willing to disclose those secrets, then earning the trust of those people, forced me to explore the city. In the end, and because of our life at the time, we met all kinds of people. Some of those people I intentionally met to help me with my work. Others, we met by chance.

Throughout the first months, though, I struggled with finding that balance—the same struggle that would resurface time and time again with every move.

Exploring the corners of Paris was fascinating in itself, but it also helped me learn the routes I needed to take to conduct an operation. Areas inside the Boulevard Périphérique—the twenty arrondissements (or districts) of Paris—were congested, too congested for an effective clandestine meeting. Just outside, however, in one of the many close suburbs, I could find exactly what I was looking for. Issy les Moulineau was one of those spots.

It was a cool autumn, midweek early evening. I left the Embassy at a reasonable late afternoon hour. I had several "errands" to run that eventually led me to the end of the Line 12 metro and the Mairie d'Issy stop. From there, I walked at a relatively brisk pace, stopping first at a café for a sparkling water and to watch the passersby for ten minutes. I continued walking several blocks, stopping at two small shops before turning right onto Passage Saint Jean and descending some steps to Rue de la Glacière. I was right on time to meet my agent, a Libyan who was to pick me up in his vehicle for our meeting—a technique we called a "reverse car pickup." It was our regularly scheduled bimonthly meeting, and I had some follow-up questions to ask him from our last meeting. He was a senior official in his government and had inside knowledge of the players in line for leadership positions.

But…he wasn't there. I waited about ninety seconds, then continued down Rue de la Glacière and away from the pickup spot. Things had just become a bit complicated. We had an alternate plan, of course. I always ensured we did. I would return to the spot in exactly one hour. If Mahmoud still wasn't there, I'd move to Plan C. What was more worrisome right then was that I had planned the evening to the minute and had fully intended to make it to an informal presentation at Claire's nursery school. They were having a celebration to acknowledge the new school year, and all the children were participating. I knew Joe was ready to handle it all, but I so wanted to be there too. In the end, my meeting with Mahmoud happened exactly an hour later. He had simply been caught in traffic and so knew to move to the alternate plan when he realized he wouldn't make our initial designated time. Unfortunately, I didn't get home until after Joe and Claire. Claire was already getting ready for her bedtime story.

This was my life now, I realized. I couldn't always count on being where I wanted to be. But I absolutely had to focus on my agents and the mission. That was the priority.

My work was constant, every minute of every day. I couldn't afford to rest or to let my guard down. It was as though I couldn't take a break. I had to be ready to take advantage of any situation that presented itself. Everything I said and did had to be said and done with forethought. Every interaction had to be measured and carefully examined. Nothing could be taken for granted. Every walk in the Parc Monceau or along the Seine, every visit to the banlieues or during an excursion outside Paris, I was working to find that next nugget of information, that inroad to a stream of information. All the while, I would be listening for and watching for a threat against me—any situation where someone might be trying to find out what I was really doing in Paris.

Over time, we came to know the city better, its streets and landmarks, its look and feel. We became entrenched in its daily routine. As the days passed, there was little distinction between my work and my family life. It was all part of the same journey. Still, Joe and I knew we had this enormous responsibility of ensuring our daughter learned how to acclimate in an international setting and that she (and subsequently all our children) learned right from wrong, to be thankful and appreciative, to be curious and excited about everything around them, to be thoughtful and considerate.

As our family continued to grow through the years, everything became a bit more complicated. Fitting our many belongings into suitcases, herding everyone on and off planes, finding a taxi to fit us all, making decisions that were good for everyone—it was a lot to juggle. But despite complications and unexpected hassles, these trips and our lives really did become richer with every move and every child.

As a mom, I came to expect a lot from my children. I discovered the difference between employees and children was that the latter couldn't "escape." They *had* to listen to me. I was right there, in front of them, all the time. In the end, though, like the rookie CIA officers I supervised later in my career, I hoped that they, too, would learn a few things that might keep them out of danger and help them grow into independent thinkers and mature adults.

If things were so good, I wondered, why was I always so stressed? Why was I so worried, so concerned about life, balance, and my family? Why did I always have so much on my mind?

Finding good daycare, for example, was mentally exhausting. I was working. Joe was working. We didn't have family or friends we could rely upon. Our very first effort in Paris to find care for Claire—a stay-at-home mom at the housing unit in Boulogne where we stayed temporarily—was a disaster. It didn't last long. Claire cried inconsolably every day. It was heart-wrenching. I wanted to start my new job and feel good about it. Yet, every day, as I was trying to learn my new assignment, I knew Claire was miserable. My days at the office became interminable.

Next, we hired a young girl from West Africa named Odile. That, too, was short-lived. After only a couple of weeks, Odile suddenly told us she was sick and could no longer work. Again, we were at a loss. We just wanted a safe, nurturing situation for Claire. We were under a time constraint. Everything seemed to be falling apart.

After several weeks, once we moved into our apartment in the seventh arrondissement, we had the brilliant idea to advertise for a short-term nanny at the American Church located just across the Seine. We planned to put Claire in a local nursery school as soon as the school year began. We found exactly the type of person we were looking for and settled into a routine with our new babysitter. Liliana and her husband Sead, both from Bosnia, had recently escaped the devastating war in Sarajevo. They became much, much more than temporary babysitters to us. From the moment we met, we became close and, subsequently, lifelong friends.

Once Claire started nursery school, we developed our morning routine of walking Claire to La Crèche Municipal, where she'd spend the day. After greeting Mademoiselle Annie, a warm, effusive, but no-nonsense woman with a huge smile, Claire would deposit her pacifier or as she called it, her "paci," in the bowl and take her place in a little toddler-sized chair next to her friends Clementine and Pascal.

One day, as Joe looked up at all the apartment buildings towering over the courtyard of the crèche, he asked Annie if the residents minded the noise from the children when they played outside. Annie just chuckled and, without any hesitation, said, "All those residents are just happy to be living in the seventh, and some of them are happy just to be alive." There were far more wealthy octogenarians per square meter around us at that moment than anywhere else.

After ensuring Claire was well ensconced in the crèche, Joe and I walked a few more meters along Rue de Grenelle and descended into the La Tour Maubourg metro station. We took opposite trains and finished our morning commutes at our respective offices.

Joe's path to work, when he walked directly to his office, was a stroll under the Eiffel Tower at the end of the Champs de Mars, crossing Place du Trocadéro and turning right onto Avenue Kléber. He walked past all the tourists, feeling confidently like a true Parisian.

During our strolls with Claire, the toy store on Rue de l'Exposition, with its blue-framed windows and puzzles lined up on the shelves inside, faded from years of the sun beating down on them, was a favorite stop of ours. While Adrienne waited patiently outside, Joe would pick out a little something for Claire. The bookstore further along the same street, with its piles of books stacked on tables on the sidewalk in front, also drew Joe inside to see more. There, too, he always managed to find a new children's book—in French—for Claire to add to her collection.

As Claire's little library of French and English books grew, so did her vocabulary in both languages. During this year in Paris, she also became more mature, and her sunny disposition blossomed. Even as a toddler, Claire always wore a confident smile. She was happy. Was it life in Paris that made her round cheeks glow and her brown eyes sparkle? Was it being surrounded by interesting people all day? Was it that all her senses were heightened because so much was always happening around her?

Claire was the perfect first child to be on assignment with us. She loved adventure and exploration as much as we did and was well-behaved and interested as we saw new places and met new people. Together, we explored the Rodin Museum housed in an old hotel surrounded by a park full of sculptures and the Musee d'Orsay, a former train station now filled with Impressionist paintings. We rode the touristy but scenic Bateaux Mouches. We discovered the Musee du Vin on Rue des Eaux in the sixteenth arrondissement, an old cellar with vaulted ceilings dating from the fourteenth century when the place was an abbey.

We spent a long weekend touring the museums and the dramatic beaches of Normandy. Though Claire didn't yet understand the significance of where we were standing, we knew that somehow, the powerful emotions we were feeling would rub off on her. The entire year of 1994, the same year we lived in Paris, was a commemoration of fifty years since the Liberation of France on D-day, June 6, 1944. The whole area had an unfortunate circus-like atmosphere with trinkets and memorabilia for sale at every corner, when, in fact, what really happened on that beach in 1944 was horrific.

Over nine thousand American soldiers are buried at the American Cemetery atop a cliff overlooking Omaha Beach. We hurried past the stalls selling nonsense, saddened by the commercialization of it all. Though she was only two, Claire seemed to sense it was not the right time to ask us to buy her anything. It was a somber but dramatic moment of experiencing history, especially as we understood that fifty years had not been that long ago.

Every few months, we shopped at a large NATO military base across the border in Belgium at the Supreme Headquarters of the Allied Powers of Europe (SHAPE) in Mons. We stocked up on chocolate chips, instant oatmeal, and frozen waffles—all the American treats. One beautiful autumn Saturday, we traveled there for the afternoon since it was only a couple of hours away by car.

By that time, Liliana had been regularly babysitting Claire for several weeks. Liliana and Sead were going to spend the day together watching our little girl. Though we had only known them for a short while, we trusted our new friends completely, plus we weren't going on a long excursion. We would be back before dinner. So, after a full day of shopping, and with our car packed tight with groceries and a few presents for Claire, we crossed back into France, heading home. We called the apartment to let Liliana and Sead know we were on our way.

There was no answer.

We called again…and again and again. We must have tried fifty times to reach them, dialing and redialing every few minutes. With one hand on the redial button of an early-generation portable phone, I kept urging Joe to drive faster and faster, pleading for him to take advantage of the autoroute that had no speed limit.

We were certain we would find the apartment empty and Claire gone.

Finally inside the Boulevard Périphérique, Joe negotiated the small streets, wheeling through intersections. We screeched to a stop in front of our building, not caring that it wasn't a real parking spot, fumbled with the keys to get the large entrance door of our building open, raced to the third floor, taking the steps two at a time, and almost crashed the door down as we ran into the apartment.

Everything was quiet. Claire and Liliana were at Claire's little alphabet table playing teatime with her dolls. Sead was sitting in a nearby chair sketching as he gazed out the window onto the Eiffel Tower. Adrienne was asleep on the carpet.

"Why didn't you answer the phone?!" Joe and I asked breathlessly in unison.

"It never rang," Liliana and Sead both said in tandem.

"How can that be?" I lunged for Claire, and Joe grabbed the receiver. The phone never rang because the telephone on the front table had been unplugged, probably knocked aside by Adrienne's oh-so-graceful tail.

We slumped on the couch, embarrassed. Claire looked at us, wondering why we were in such a hurry and why we were yelling. We apologized profusely. Thankfully, Liliana and Sead immediately forgave our outburst. We had been frantic. It wasn't a good feeling at all—and this was with only one child!

Why am I always on edge? I asked myself later once I had calmed down. Was it worrying about my child being in a foreign land with people we didn't know very well? Or was it because, deep down, I knew I couldn't really control everything?

Not long after we met them, we learned Liliana and Sead's story. The more time we spent together, the more we began to understand the heartache and suffering they had endured in leaving their war-torn home of Sarajevo.

Liliana was Serbian. Sead was Bosnian. They met in Sarajevo when they were teenagers in high school. They got married and were destined to live happily ever after. Then the war started. Sarajevo became a literal hellhole. "Sniper Alley," once a main commercial thoroughfare through Sarajevo, became a death zone. In 1994, as Sarajevo fell deeper into despair, Liliana and Sead knew they had to escape the devastating situation developing in Sarajevo and throughout all Bosnia-Herzegovina. Given the constant shelling of the city, the only "safe" exit was through an underground passage leading from the airport. Together, leaving families and friends behind, Liliana and Sead got out and eventually made it to Italy, where they took refuge temporarily with some distant family members. They couldn't stay there very long and eventually continued on to Paris.

Liliana had a wealthy cousin in Paris whom she thought she could rely upon to help get them settled and start a new life. She was very wrong. They were treated shabbily by him, to the point where he suggested Liliana sing in the metro to earn money. Liliana's father had aided this cousin when he was younger, but when his help was needed most by Liliana, he simply chose not to reciprocate. Liliana and Sead arrived in Paris with literally only the clothes on their backs. They found a tiny room the size of a single dormitory room in the fifteenth arrondissement where they ate, slept, and lived.

With sparkling emerald eyes and a brilliant smile, Liliana was beautiful, elegant, gregarious, full of emotion, full of life, and so very kind. Sead was tall and handsome but also funny, creative, thoughtful, considerate, and an exceptional artist. They were a perfect match. Theirs was a true love story—the life they had begun and the horrors they survived together were nothing short of extraordinary.

Though they were political refugees with every reason to be in France, it took years for them to obtain French residency status. They had one son, Andrea, who was born in France. Like his father, he was a brilliant artist. He studied architecture and engineering in Paris and is now in high demand for his creative and technical expertise.

Sead passed away in 2013, after a difficult struggle with cancer. We remember Sead sitting at our dinner table or out with us at a favorite café, smiling brilliantly, cracking jokes, and laughing with us. In fact, just saying his name reminds us of some of our happiest moments. Sead was like that—his presence alone made you smile.

It is these incredible, lifelong, irreplaceable relationships that we experienced in large part because my work took us to spectacular places which provided us the opportunity to meet amazing people. How else would we have met people like Liliana and Sead—people with such heartfelt and personal experiences who were willing to share their stories and themselves with us? They were born on the other side of the globe, saw complete devastation and tragedy in their lives, and yet somehow, during that year in Paris, we found ourselves in the same little corner of the world as them. In 2010, when Claire decided to attend college in Paris, it was only because Liliana and Sead were still there that we felt comfortable with our daughter so far away.

I have a memory of our beautiful apartment in Paris that I bury deep. It's almost too painful to recall. When I'm forced to speak about it, a bit of panic sets in, and I once again question my ability as a mother. Joe and I were in our small kitchen one weekend morning making a coffee. Claire was playing with some puzzles on the floor of her room—or so we thought. The doorbell rang. Joe and I looked at each other with a questioning look. We usually didn't get unexpected callers. Joe went to answer the door and opened it to a woman yelling in French. It took a moment for me to comprehend that she was furiously yelling, "*La fille, la fille!*" She turned around and ran down the stairs. We followed. We pounded through the heavy front door and into a throng of people on the sidewalk, all looking up at our apartment. We followed their intent stares. There was Claire—standing OUTSIDE the balcony grate on a small sliver of cement!

Without thinking, I turned and ran back into the building. For some miraculous reason, the large, iron door that usually closed and locked as one left, had remained ajar. I ran up the spiral staircase taking the steps two at a time. I crashed through the door of our apartment that we had also left open, burst into the bedroom overlooking the street, saw the balcony a few feet in front of me, and in one long stride came up behind Claire and scooped her up and over the balcony railing into my arms. I sunk down on the bedroom floor, unable to control my breathing. Joe came in right behind me, and we knew we had just witnessed a miracle.

The wonderful group of French neighbors below had been trying to position themselves in the event Claire fell so that they could hopefully catch her before she landed on the pavement. They had been calling up to her, trying to coax her back through the grate.

Why had we been so distracted? Why were we so assured nothing could go wrong? Was I too tired from thinking about my work that I couldn't focus on my family?

Not long after arriving in Paris, I helped expand the international clubs of my alma mater, the University of Notre Dame. Though Notre Dame's alumni network is vast, there was no club in Paris. I set about changing that. It didn't take long to find all kinds of former students and friends of Notre Dame in the city, many of whom loved the idea of getting together to reminisce and share stories and camaraderie. I tracked down and coordinated outings for the group, hosted ND cocktail parties at our apartment, and arranged to host the university's president, Father Monk Malloy, at a beautiful, old, vaulted underground restaurant. We were a fun, somewhat eclectic group bound by a common and proud background.

Joe also found his own niche in Paris when he became a member of the "Phenix" Motorcycle Club based in the suburbs. A secretary at the US Embassy had read about the group in a local newspaper and knew Joe had a Harley-Davidson. She pointed Joe in their direction. Joe rode his bike with the group for hours on the weekends, learning the roads in and around the city, often ending up at Thérèse's Café in one of Paris's suburbs for a late afternoon beer with his new friends.

On one weeklong motorcycle excursion, we again left Claire with Liliana and Sead and rode from France through England and into Wales. We started out by meeting our "Phenix" friends just outside Paris in the suburb of Boulogne, then together rode to Cherbourg and took the overnight ferry to Portsmouth. We rode to Stonehenge and then crossed into Wales, where we stopped at King Henry V's birthplace, Monmouth Castle.

Our return route took us to the White Cliffs of Dover, then onto the ferry from Dover to Calais. We rode to Agincourt, the site of the famous October 1415 battle in the Hundred Years War where the English, led by King Henry V, were victorious over the French. Over and over, through the years, we've listened to Shakespeare's version of Henry V's moving speech to his friends on the battlefield that day. It is this same speech that I would hear a few years later from my commander in Sarajevo as we all huddled together on Christmas morning, proud of what we were there to do.

We moved Joe's seven-hundred-pound Super Glide Harley-Davidson across the Atlantic to every country in which we lived. Though it took up a large part of our allotted weight, it was worth it. Joe rode his bike everywhere, almost every day. It was also a great conversation piece and made him some great friends.

Once, he rode up to a police checkpoint, slowly, of course, and with a small bit of trepidation as he didn't speak the local language. As a diplomat, he didn't really expect to be stopped. Unfortunately, though, not just one but five policemen, all standing together, gestured for him to pull over. One by one, they began to encircle his motorcycle. At first very concerned, Joe quickly realized that all they wanted to do was admire his bike! The local police force didn't often see a large American motorcycle on the small streets of their country.

Joe was proud of his bike. He loved to meet new people wherever we lived and learn a bit of the local language when he was able. He could do all this simply by riding his motorcycle to his office. Joe sometimes mounted a camera on the handlebars and filmed his commute, as well as his forays into the countryside.

On this first overseas assignment to Paris, Joe watched as I worked my craft—meeting and talking to people, then meeting certain ones again. Watching me, he quickly learned what my job was all about. Without me even telling him who I was meeting with and where or why I was having those meetings, he understood. He didn't need to know how long I would be gone each time I left the house or where I was. He knew not to ask questions. He knew not to worry when I was out late at night. He knew not to wonder why I insisted we take a certain route to the store. He knew not to argue when I said I couldn't be somewhere for the children. He knew not to expect regular telephone check-ins when I was traveling. He knew that if there was an emergency and he absolutely had to reach me, there was an official way to do it.

A spouse willing to understand this life, the importance of the work, and the idiosyncrasies of this kind of job, is not easy to find. I needed it, though, to be successful in my work *and* as a mom.

Joe didn't complain. He didn't get jealous. Rather, he embraced the life we had. He soaked up the acquaintances and friendships we made.

We were still in Paris when I learned I was pregnant with baby number two. We didn't know at the time if our next child was a boy or girl. We looked back over the past year and what we thought was our perfect situation—just the three of us, Adrienne, and a life in Paris—and wondered what the next year would bring.

Then, it all ended…suddenly and unexpectedly. It was always part of the "game." If counterintelligence concerns dictated or operations were endangered of becoming exposed, officers would be sent home. It made sense. It was ultimately for the safety of the officers and their families, as well as the safety of our operations. I knew this.

But then it happened to us. At first, I was told my office would try to find a way to let me keep working in Europe. It soon became apparent, though, that that wasn't going to happen.

We tried to fit in as much as possible of the life we were experiencing, knowing we were soon leaving it all behind. In the end, we only had one year in France. Our flexibility and ability to dodge and weave was truly being tested.

From our perspective, our perfect life was over. Claire was speaking French. I loved my job. My husband loved his job with Booz Allen Hamilton. The city was magical. We had wonderful friends. Then, throgh a counterintelligence flap, a situation having nothing to do with us, we were expected to pack up and leave. We also needed to create an explanation for our families. Except for my father, no one really knew exactly what we were doing in Paris.

We faced another difficult transition, and I asked myself if I should be working for a different organization in a safer, less volatile situation or if I should completely adjust my plans and my goals, if I was even doing the right thing for my family. Joe and I wondered what was next, what prospects waited around the corner, and what opportunities or troubles lay ahead. It was especially frustrating for Joe to have to quit yet another job after only one year and move again so quickly. This life, at times, seemed artificial.

Sometimes, it didn't seem worth it.

It all seemed unfair. The day we left Paris was heartbreaking. We wondered if we would ever be as happy again. Another baby was on the way. But where were we going to settle? What jobs would we have? What friends would we make? Life seemed daunting, disconcerting, and uncertain.

Chapter Seven

The Turkey Experience

Turkey
1995

In late March 1995, Joe, Claire, and I flew Turkish Airlines from Paris Orly Airport to Istanbul for a weeklong getaway. We had tickets and an itinerary from a tour company that called themselves "Le Grand Specialiste de la Turkie." Our brilliant idea to take off to Turkey and not fully research the plan beforehand meant we were slapped with a fine as soon as we entered the arrivals terminal in Istanbul for not having a visa in our passports authorizing entry into the country. After spending a few lire and signing a few papers, we left the airport, stood in line for a taxi, and headed into the city!

Istanbul stimulated all our senses in a dramatic way. From the moment we landed, we knew it was a different kind of place. The colors were intense. The aromatic scents from the spice market enthralled us and their exotic, magical fragrances seemed to follow us everywhere. All day, every day, we heard the rumbling sounds from the horns of boats and barges on the Bosphorus, the famous waterway that forms part of the unique boundary between Asia and Europe.

The day we visited the famous Blue Mosque, one of the most well-known and dramatic of the city's landmarks, the sky was clear and bright blue, almost as if giving us a personal invitation to walk inside the holy place. The thin minarets stretched into that azure sky high above its red granite and marble exterior walls. We experienced all this even before stepping across the threshold and into an immense space where we were suddenly surrounded by the millions and millions of striking cobalt tiles that made up its interior walls.

The vivid red Turkish flag flew, it seemed, from every building and off of every market stall crisscrossing the halls of the Grand Bazaar; blue, red, and white tiles were crafted into the yellow mosaic ceiling in the halls, and reds, blues, golds, and greens spilled out of dozens and dozens of carpet stores as if the carpets themselves were beckoning people in.

I had no need of any spices, but the labyrinth of stalls, each displaying bushels of spices in more greens, reds, yellows, and copper colors was simply impossible to leave once I was inside.

We tried to identify the mélange of sounds we heard as we wandered through the streets and into the plazas—the calls of the merchants inviting prospective clients in for tea, the lively consonants of the Turkish language, and the waiters in the restaurants encouraging us to try their specialties.

Even though the sidewalks were crumbling in spots and the streets were overcrowded with cars and people (making our journey with the stroller a huge challenge), Istanbul, this "pearl of the Orient," completely captivated us. We felt warmly welcomed and excited at the new experiences around every corner. Even Claire, from her spot in the stroller at the level of everyone's knees, was constantly entertained by the sights, sounds, and colors.

We stayed at the Hotel Festival in the Çemberlitaş district, only ten minutes from the amazing sites of the Blue Mosque, the Hagia Sophia Grand Mosque (formerly an Orthodox Church, then a Catholic cathedral, then a museum, and finally, again, a mosque), and the Grand Bazaar. It was a simple hotel decorated in the Ottoman style, so it felt right. After our first full day exploring the neighborhoods, the food, and the architecture of this magical city, all three of us were ready to collapse for the night. We tucked Claire, still a toddler, into the extra bed in the room. We had no energy for a story that night. In any case, she was already sound asleep when we turned back around to check on her. Soon, we too fell asleep in the comfortable double bed next to her. We slept with the window open, in part because it was a warm night, but we also wanted to fall asleep listening to the melodic sounds of the bustling street below.

Suddenly, a shrill, ear-piercing alarm sounded, jolting us out of bed. Claire started howling. *Where are we? What just happened?* I ran to Claire's side and picked her up. She had wet the bed and was a mess from the scare. It took us a few minutes to understand what we'd just heard and a few minutes more to realize that we were fools for not expecting the Islamic call to prayer at some point during the night. We knew how Muslims worshiped. The call to prayer, recited by a muezzin or an official of every mosque over loudspeakers installed on the tall, slender minaret towers of the mosque, occurs five times daily, every day. We had also seen a mosque standing grandly outside our hotel window as we settled into our room. None of that prepared us for the booming, rhythmic chants that woke us that first very early morning in Istanbul.

A few moments later, now wide awake, the three of us stood at the window watching the early morning activities on the street below—the merchants running across the narrow streets with trays of Turkish coffees, doors of shops being rolled up, and the blazing orange sun rising over the horizon in the distance. We were embarrassed for our lapse in knowing the cultural norms, and it reinforced the fact that we had so much more to learn.

We got ourselves together, dressed Claire, and gave her the banana we had saved from our stop at the market the day before. Then, we headed out to look for a cup of thick, strong Turkish coffee to start our day. At the corner of the street, a block from our hotel, Claire and I sat at a small plastic table outside a tiny café while Joe went in and bought several pastries dripping with honey and two very small, very strong coffees. We sat watching the morning activities start up around us as we tore off pieces of the sweet pastry to hand to Claire who sat complacently in her stroller by our side.

That week, we sailed along the Bosphorus, luxuriated in a hammam, drank tea in the old city, and, of course, shopped for carpets. Istanbul was known for its carpets with their unique, sharply colored weaves and brilliant, meaningful motifs.

Near the old bazaar in the center of Istanbul, we visited a shop that was recommended to us by friends. There was a whole process to buying a carpet in Turkey. We learned along the way.

First came the introductions. The merchants in the particular carpet store we chose to visit had worked with many Americans over the years and so understood what we were hoping to find. The two owners of the shop offered us seats and served tea. It was comfortable. We felt we were the only ones that mattered to them. Claire climbed up on a pile of carpets on one side of the tiny room and sat like a princess looking down upon us.

We chatted about our visit to Turkey thus far, about our interests, our families, and how we ended up in this tiny store in the middle of the Old Bazaar. After almost thirty minutes, following the lead of the merchants, we started to talk about carpets. No one seemed in a hurry, and no one seemed to have an agenda. The two merchants were proud of their livelihood and wanted us to enjoy the whole experience. Another intersection of cultures: the Turkish way—friendly chatter, tea, unhurried conversation—and the American way, wanting to rush through the process, trying to get a good deal, concern that our baby daughter didn't get in the merchant's way or fall off the pile of carpets and hurt herself, anxious not to keep other potential clients waiting.

In the end, we knew we couldn't really stress about which carpet was the perfect one. Instead, we decided to choose ones we'd like to see on our floors at home from among the thousands of carpets. So what if it wasn't the "best" deal—whatever that meant. We knew we would leave with beautiful, genuine Turkish carpets that would adorn every place we lived from that point forward.

We took the wise suggestions of the owners of the shop, our two new best friends, and left with three Ushak carpets (named after one of the larger towns in Western Anatolia). They were wool on wool, hand-knotted in a double Turkish knot, vegetable dyed, and naturally colored. The largest one, mostly red, had stylized flowers and animal motifs throughout. We purchased a red runner with medallion designs joined together with other designs of chains. The serpents and crosses on this carpet signified protection specifically against the evil eye - which we thought might do us some good! The stars signified happiness, and the comb motifs signified good luck. All positive, useful wishes. We also purchased a small, navy-blue carpet with a design of tulips, crosses, houses (symbolizing a village), a wolf's mouth (more protection), and a woman with her hands on her hips (signifying fertility and motherhood). All three carpets were readied and packaged for us to check as baggage on our return flight to Paris. We paid with what is now "old Turkish lira," which came to be known only a few years later as the world's least valuable currency. Maybe we got a good deal after all.

A short walk from the Grand Bazaar, we stopped at one of the seemingly hundreds of restaurants hocking their seafood dishes. We couldn't really tell one from another but decided since we were close to so many bodies of water—the Mediterranean, the Aegean, the Black Sea, and the Sea of Marmara—we couldn't go wrong with fresh fish. We were waved into one of the establishments and sat down at a table near the front so we could watch the bustling street. Before we could get comfortable, though, we were ushered to the large tank in the back of the restaurant to "pick what we wanted." Standing like two misplaced, confused tourists, we eventually and very hesitantly pointed at a big black fish swimming around, then quickly sat back down at our table to wait.

Then came dinner—not two simple seafood meals but an entire fish on a huge platter, professionally laid down before us with a flourish by the hurried, apron-clad waiter. The whole fish was cleaned and ready to eat, but every part of it seemed intact as the eyes glared at us from one side of the dish. Luckily, the waiter had already dashed off to serve another table before we could utter an exasperated sound or even ask for an explanation.

Claire was still trying to find words to create complete sentences, but her grimace said it all. She pointed at the fish's head and made a muffled groan of disgust. Realizing what we had just agreed to with a gesture of our fingers at the fish tank, we chuckled. We looked around at the tables near us, everyone animatedly enjoying their meals. We composed ourselves and began to slowly nibble around the head and eyes. When the waiter eventually returned to clear our plates, he had a look of understanding on his face. It seemed he had often seen foreign tourists react the same way to the restaurant's specialties.

From Istanbul, we flew south to Antalya, a resort city on Turkey's southwest Mediterranean coast. We had planned for a weekend of sun and sand after exploring the corners of busy, congested, lively Istanbul. The sea was a sparkling blue, and the hotel had an expansive pool surrounded by tall swaying palm trees…but it was March, and we had dramatically miscalculated the weather. It was cold. Too cold to swim and too cold to even wander on the beach. So, we stood on the small balcony of our hotel room, protected from the wind by piles of blankets, and gazed somewhat longingly at the clear turquoise water stretching ahead.

We were about twelve kilometers from the center of Antalya, too far to explore on foot. So we ate at the hotel restaurant and settled in to relax and, at least, enjoy the view. We were glad to be close to the beach and on vacation and wanted to enjoy our time there…for as long as it lasted.

Chapter Eight

From Stateside to Sarajevo

South Central US
1996

Another move. Another time to start all over again. After an extraordinary year in Paris where every day we experienced something new and where around every corner was a new challenge, followed by a brief but colorful vacation in Istanbul, we were now stateside once again all too quickly.

Suddenly, our life seemed so ordinary. My career had been upended. It was tough to get excited about anything during those first days back in America. We didn't know anyone in the hot, very southern state in the United States where we had landed. We didn't know what to expect. We couldn't stop thinking about how educational, fun, and eye-opening our year in Paris had been for Claire, how inspiring it had been for Joe's career, and how full, rich, and dramatic our life had been. But all that was in the past. Reluctantly, we settled into a routine back in the US. We were new to the neighborhood, new in the church, new at the playground, and new at Claire's daycare.

While it took some time, we ultimately made this new place special too. We were welcomed by people who became good friends. We learned our way around the clean, well-planned streets. We discovered cultural hideaways and trails through the hillsides. We joined other couples with young children to explore parks and watering holes throughout and around the city.

The biggest gift we received during these two years back in the US was our second child, Kyle, a happy and easygoing, bouncing baby boy.

I was fortunate to be able to take a few months off to spend with Kyle and Claire.

As Kyle grew, he and his big sister spent hours in the playroom loft on the second floor of our house. Claire showed Kyle how to prepare meals in her pretend kitchen, and together they created brilliant, original works of art. Claire told Kyle where to sit, what book they would read, and what game they would play. She told him when they would go outside and when they were going to stay inside and play house. Kyle was happy. He readily complied with Claire's every instruction.

As the spring of 1996 turned into summer and then autumn, the US presidential election started heating up. Bob Dole retired from the US Senate to devote his full attention to running for president as the Republican candidate. The incumbent, President Bill Clinton, was running for re-election on the Democratic ticket. It looked like the race could be a close one. Both parties held their conventions in July. Political news dominated the conversation. Iraq's Saddam Hussein was encroaching on the Kurds. The US attacked Iraq with cruise missiles to make it clear America was not pleased. Most countries backed the US except for France and a few Arab nations.

There was a lot going on out there in the world, and I occasionally felt left out of it.

I was living a fun, contented life as a full-time mom, taking advantage of every single day of my maternity leave. Together with my new friends, we loaded up our kids and headed out to explore. We visited new, fun places and experienced some beautiful scenery—rolling hills, huge green pastures, rivers, lakes, clear refreshing springs, fragrant fields of bluebonnets, and museums with all kinds of hands-on projects that taught us and the kids about this new part of America where we lived. Time passed quickly.

That first summer with Kyle, the weather was unbearably hot and sticky. State authorities pleaded with residents to conserve water. Joe and I were unfazed by the extreme temperatures. It always seemed so hot there that, frankly, we couldn't tell any difference between a regular day and a record-breaking hot one!

We never stopped looking for new places to discover. We swam in the local spring-fed swimming hole, attended outdoor concerts, toured the local university, climbed trails, hiked mountains, camped, and went tubing in the rivers of the local state parks, all with two toddlers in tow.

We walked around the lively, music-filled downtown area, experienced new restaurants, soaked up the history, and reveled in the part that this hot, southern region had in America's story. It was just Joe and me and our two tiny children. It was easy to get up and go. Life was still an adventure, and we wanted to take advantage of what was in front of us.

After months of this unscheduled, casual, idyllic life, I found myself back at work. I forced myself to develop a routine. I had to get into some kind of rhythm and get organized. I left the house in the morning knowing what I had to accomplish every day and what I had to tackle every night when I got home. I didn't travel very often during those initial days back in the office. I thought staying close to home would make establishing a routine a bit easier. We had found a good daycare for Kyle and a good preschool for Claire. Using his electrical engineering skills, Joe quickly found a fulfilling job with IBM. Everything fit nicely into the day or the week. Things were more or less running smoothly.

In August of Kyle's first year, he took his inaugural plane ride to New York to see family—Grandma and Grandpa, Grand-père, aunts, uncles, and cousins. We started planning for his christening, wanting to get Kyle baptized before his first birthday. We had already waited longer than I wanted. Work had been busy, but it was also becoming a bit predictable, which, all things considered, seemed like a welcome change.

Sarajevo
1996-1997

In October, I saw a need to help in a region of the world I wanted to understand better. CIA's Office of Military Affairs put out a call for an operations officer to complete a team of three to become part of the US military's contingent to NATO in Sarajevo, Bosnia. It would be very much out of my comfort zone, but that's what excited me.

Yet, I had two small children to care for at home. I debated with myself, weighing the pros and cons.

Joe broke the tie, encouraging me to take the assignment. He knew I was anxious to get out to the foreign field again.

We moved up the date of Kyle's christening—an important milestone on our calendars—and I scrambled to prepare everything for a four-month trip to the Balkans, an area just recovering from the aftermath of a war.

On the morning that I was due to leave for Sarajevo, our family and some close friends, acting as proxies for Kyle's godparents, gathered at our local Catholic church for Kyle's christening. Kyle wore the same cream-colored, satin christening gown with a delicate, rose-colored ribbon that I had made for Claire. It was an important day for us. I tried to take comfort in staying in the moment that day. Sitting in the front row holding Kyle in my arms, I gazed at the stained-glass windows of the modern church that had become so familiar to us in only a few months. As I thought about the ritual of water and oil to be poured by the priest over my son's tiny head, I felt a complete sense of calm that he was now totally and completely under God's protection.

Still, this sense of comfort was juxtaposed with my anxiousness about getting on a plane later that very same day and traveling thousands of miles away from my home to a country ravaged by war and leaving my baby boy, my little girl, and my husband behind.

During the Mass, I thought about how our lives were changing and how they would be different over the next few months. Sitting in the pew listening to Father Williams, I prayed that all would be well with Joe and the children, our extended family, and our friends and neighbors, all of whom I knew would be supporting Joe while I was so far away. I knew I was leaving my family behind in a safe place, but I also realized that I was heading for the unknown.

This wasn't a simple overseas jaunt. Sarajevo was still reeling from the effects of war. The city had been bombarded relentlessly until just a few months prior, and I was walking into the middle of it. This wasn't a tourist trip where I'd have an opportunity to explore the area and see the sights. I was going to be part of a NATO effort to bring peace to the region. Of course, I wasn't doing this alone, but I took my part seriously. I knew a lot would be asked of me, that I would be working long hours, and that I wouldn't know what my family was doing day to day. It was a daunting task.

When I arrived in Bosnia, I found myself at the site of a crisis that the world had watched in horror, one where ruthless dictators, responsible for unspeakable atrocities, were still being chased. Yet, somehow, despite the barbaric experiences the city had witnessed, I saw a demonstration of the power and resilience of human nature. The tragic events began in 1992, only a few years prior. I could not discuss my work with my family, but what I saw day to day throughout Sarajevo would forever affect the way I interacted with others, especially my family.

The streets were empty. Stores were shuttered. Though bullets were no longer raining down on the city center, few people were outside. The locals I met were downcast and sullen. The families I interacted with spent hours talking about how their city *used* to be—how everyone got along, how lively the place was, and how proud they were to be Bosnian. When I interacted with people my age or with moms and their children, I struggled to understand how people "just like me" managed to live a life so very, very different from mine. Theirs was a life where every day was a struggle, where neighbors had become enemies, where their beautiful city was now riddled with mortar shells and bullets. While my children did not see what I saw, I was certain that the effect this experience had on me would ultimately somehow be passed on to them.

Before the war, Sarajevo was a beautiful, cosmopolitan city. Its mystical landscape was dotted with Byzantine domes, cathedral spires, and Islamic minarets, demonstrating how perfectly the city's multicultural canvas co-existed. It was on the world stage in 1984 as host of the Winter Olympics. But beginning in April 1992, it was pummeled and battered relentlessly for three and a half years.

Following Bosnia and Herzegovina's Declaration of Independence from Yugoslavia in 1992, the Bosnian Serbs wanted to create a new state for themselves that would include the Bosniak majority areas. They were defiant. They were also bellicose and cruel. They encircled Sarajevo and began a horrific siege of the city. Serbs hid in the hills and in high-rise buildings surrounding and throughout the city and relentlessly, indiscriminately shot at anything that moved using mortar shells and sniper fire.

People risked their lives just to cross from one side of the main thoroughfare, "Sniper Alley," to the other to get home. Many never made it. In 1993, a one-kilometer tunnel was dug that ran under the Sarajevo airport and was the city's only link with the outside world. Supplies, weapons, and ammunition were smuggled in as the city had been cut off from all food or medicine. People used the one way out to escape certain death or, at a minimum, starvation.

This included our good friends, Liliana and Sead. They escaped their well-loved but battered city in the spring of 1994 and arrived in Paris that summer.

The Dayton Peace Agreement ended the war. It was signed at Wright Patterson Air Force Base in Dayton, Ohio, in November 1995 and formally signed in Paris on December 14th. On February 29, 1996, the Bosnian government officially declared the siege over. Terms of the agreement included recognizing Bosnia and Herzegovina as a single state with two multiethnic entities, the Federation of

Bosnia and Herzegovina and the Republika of Srpska. The agreement also instituted a multinational peacekeeping force, international police monitors, and several international civilian bodies dedicated to rebuilding Bosnia. I was a part of the US contingent assigned to this effort. I arrived in Sarajevo not long after the siege ended.

Sarajevo already had a place in the history books as the site where World War I started with a vengeance when Archduke Franz Ferdinand, heir to the Austro-Hungarian throne, was assassinated by a Bosnian Serb named Gavrilo Princip.

Bosnia has always been a diverse country. That was its magic. Religious and ethnic differences never mattered. Rather, it was precisely those differences that created its beauty. Muslims, Orthodox and Protestant Christians, Catholics, and Jews all coexisted harmoniously. There were tall, majestic buildings, a winding river, snow-covered hills, and a myriad of people everywhere. On the banks of the river was one of Sarajevo's most impressive buildings, the National Library. It was burned to the ground in August 1992 after being hit by a mortar round. Over two million books were destroyed. It shocked me to see a historical building—once so beautiful and magnificent, looming above the river that wound through the city—now just a shell of its former self. It was as if nothing was sacred, nothing was important, and nothing in the city meant anything to those who were destroying it. Throughout the streets were large craters left behind by the shelling. Many of them were subsequently filled with a red resin substance and became known as "Sarajevo Roses." They marked the fallen who died at those spots. Each time I came upon one of these Sarajevo Roses, my heart stopped as I thought of how someone died right there just trying to walk to the market.

I had never seen so much destruction and devastation in one place. Much of my time in Sarajevo was spent at the United Nations (UN) military facility. Every day there were briefings and meetings regarding decisions and ideas on how to protect the citizens, keep war from breaking out again, and create a safe and secure environment going forward.

Traveling outside Sarajevo to the US military base in Tuzla, passing through villages and towns along the way, highlighted how much more devastating the war had been on Sarajevo than elsewhere in the country.

Just outside Sarajevo was a neighborhood known as Ilidza. There stood a resort complex that included five hotels, a restaurant, and a separate multipurpose building. In December 1995, French troops took occupation of the resort area and converted it into the headquarters of the NATO peacekeeping force IFOR (Implementation Force) and subsequently SFOR (Stabilization Force). This is where I lived and worked for four months.

We were housed in one of the former hotels, a four-story structure with almost two hundred rooms and the largest building in the complex. Accommodations were basic. The shelling of Sarajevo had only stopped a few months before my arrival. I was glad to have shelter even if we only periodically had running water, heat, and electricity. We kept our bathtubs full in case we lost complete access to water. My room held several sets of bunk beds. It was evident that the rooms had, at one time, been elegant and posh. Now, they simply provided shelter.

Two of the hotels were joined by a common reception area that led to the dining room. As we were in the UN's French Sector following Bosnia's partition, French chefs prepared three meals a day for all of us—both soldiers and civilians. The UN commanders lived with us in the same accommodations and ate at the same dining hall.

Large metal container boxes throughout the grounds housed our offices, the various National Intel Cells (NICs), the communications gear, and the portable showers and toilets. This area of Ilidza is often considered to be one of the most important places in SFOR's and Bosnia and Herzegovina's post-war history for what it represented and for the decisions made and carried out there.

Plans designed by terrorists to harm US persons or places, specifics about who was planning the attacks and when they would take place—this was the intelligence we were tasked to acquire. We sought any information about the intentions that nefarious foreign governments or foreign non-state actors had to do harm to the US. In the military world, it was this intelligence that sometimes made the difference between life and death on the battlefield. The CIA's intelligence was good. Our sources were vetted and validated, and we had confidence in our work.

My commander at the National Intelligence Support Team (NIST) was a driven, committed, no-nonsense Marine lieutenant colonel. He understood the importance of why we were there and ensured his entire command knew and understood it, too. He came into our tiny workspace several times a day to inquire about a piece of information, to pass on some important news, or just to ensure we stayed motivated. Sometimes, he would ask for follow-up on a piece of intelligence that came in that morning. Sometimes, he wanted more information on a specific lead. And sometimes, he just wanted to see if the CIA had anything new or different from what he had already heard. I had to be ready to answer his questions. His number one priority was force protection as his troops conducted the mission of keeping the peace. He knew the importance of advanced warnings of attacks and expected my team to provide information that was timely and relevant.

We spent hours scouring material, talking to our headquarters in Langley, Virginia, and meeting with other countries' NICs—all to stay aware of any threats to our military as the troops did what they needed to do to create and maintain peace in what had been a grisly environment. We knew there were still criminals, rogues, and terrorists roaming the region whose only goal was to ensure peace did *not* prevail. Iranian intelligence operatives, for example, were in Bosnia. We knew they were there, and we knew their purpose was to harm the US or other Western nations. Working with NATO intelligence groups, the US military, and local Bosnian officials, our small, three-person CIA contingent shared what we knew, what pieces were still missing and tried to provide the Generals with a comprehensive look at what was happening around us in as real-time as possible.

I wasn't on the pointy end of the spear. I was behind the scenes reading intelligence reports, talking to analysts, and researching answers to questions. It wasn't sexy work. Hours were long and, at times, tedious. But at every morning stand-up brief, when our commander called the NIC together to tell us what had occurred overnight, to highlight potential threats to our US Forces and tell us what we needed to do that day, I was revived and knew I was in the right place.

Before I left my four-year-old daughter and toddler son for what would be a long four months in this cold, far-off, war-torn city, I created huge, color-coded calendars and hung them across the wall next to the kitchen. Then, I filled in each daily block with all the necessary to-do's. This large effort included all the things I was certain were the most critical for Joe to complete each day—the essential duties and the details I wanted to make sure he didn't forget. Everything important was on those calendars, including when to cut the children's fingernails, when to schedule playdates, and what to feed the children for snacks.

If I wasn't going to be there to make sure everything got done, at least I would write it all down, in very clear terms, so there would be no mishaps. I eventually learned that only a short while after I left Joe took down all the paper calendars I had so carefully prepared and so lovingly posted. Apparently, they weren't as necessary or critical as I thought they would be. In the end, and despite my anxious thoughts, I realized that somehow, even being so far away, everything that needed to be done was getting done…and more.

I had a tough time being away from the family, probably more difficult than they had being away from me. Every night for the first week, I cried myself to sleep as I lay on the bottom bunk of my not-so-private room in an old, cold, and drafty building. *What was I thinking? Why did I leave my two young babies? Are they okay? Will they remember me when I eventually got back home?*

The days passed, and I slowly began to understand my contribution to the mission I was supporting. I would often break away from my spot in my CONEX box (an eight-by-twenty-foot metal shipping container that we retrofitted into a sort of office) and go for a run to clear my mind, contemplate my role there, and get a slight change of scenery. Even that little bit of something different, though, was complicated. Buried mines everywhere meant only certain routes could be followed. Nothing—even exercise—was easy.

Our Marine commander summoned the entire US NIC together on Christmas morning of 1996. We were all far from our families, and as we amassed on a wooden deck built on the side of one of the CONEX boxes, surrounded by dirt and snow in the middle of a fierce Balkan winter, he told us we were in this fight together and we needed to have each other's backs. He said he was there for us and reminded us of the important work we were doing. For many reasons, as I watched our NIC work, I developed a permanent respect not only for him but for all Marines and for our US military.

Then, he read us a speech that King Henry V gave to his soldiers just before they went off to fight at the Battle of Agincourt:

What's he that wishes so?
My cousin Westmoreland? No, my fair cousin;
If we are mark'd to die, we are enow
To do our country loss; and if to live,
The fewer men, the greater share of honor.
God's will! I pray thee, wish not one man more.
By Jove, I am not covetous for gold,
Nor care I who doth feed upon my cost;
It yearns me not if men my garments wear;
Such outward things dwell not in my desires.
But if it be a sin to covet honor,
I am the most offending soul alive.
No, faith, my coz, wish not a man from England.
God's peace! I would not lose so great an honor
As one man more methinks would share from me
For the best hope I have. O, do not wish one more!
Rather proclaim it, Westmoreland, through my host,

That he which hath no stomach to this fight,
Let him depart; his passport shall be made,
And crowns for convoy put into his purse;
We would not die in that man's company
That fears his fellowship to die with us.
This day is call'd the feast of Crispian.
He that outlives this day, and comes safe home,
Will stand a tip-toe when this day is nam'd,
And rouse him at the name of Crispian.
He that shall live this day, and see old age,
Will yearly on the vigil feast his neighbors,
And say "To-morrow is Saint Crispian."
Then will he strip his sleeve and show his scars,
And say "These wounds I had on Crispian's day."
Old men forget; yet all shall be forgot,
But he'll remember, with advantages,
What feats he did that day. Then shall our names,
Familiar in his mouth as household words-
Harry the King, Bedford and Exeter,
Warwick and Talbot, Salisbury and Gloucester-
Be in their flowing cups freshly rememb'red.
This story shall the good man teach his son;
And Crispin Crispian shall ne'er go by,
From this day to the ending of the world,
But we in it shall be remembered-
We few, we happy few, we band of brothers;
For he to-day that sheds his blood with me
Shall be my brother; be he ne'er so vile,
This day shall gentle his condition;
And gentlemen in England now-a-bed
Shall think themselves accurs'd they were not here,

And hold their manhoods cheap whiles any speaks
That fought with us upon Saint Crispin's day.

—William Shakespeare's *Henry V*, Act 4, Scene 3

This was long before the days of Skype, FaceTime, and WhatsApp. It was difficult to stay connected to my family. Long-distance calls home were complicated. Once a week, I stood in line at the commo truck. It was just a retrofitted pickup truck with a communications hookup on the back bed. When it was finally my turn, I hopped onto the truck, moved several layers of camouflage aside, found the correct levers, flipped some switches and, if I was lucky, I would get a link back to the US.

Calls were never lengthy, as there were always people lined up outside the truck waiting their turn. There was, of course, no video, and the connection wasn't always clear, but even this rudimentary communication somewhat helped keep the family connection alive.

I found conversations were stilted, though. I couldn't talk about what I was doing in Sarajevo. And since I wasn't doing anything besides working, I didn't have much to say at all. I didn't want to lament about missing them so much. Since we only spoke intermittently over those months, I wasn't even able to follow what was happening back home. It was a tough time—at least for me. The kids and Joe carried on with their usual routines. I, on the other hand, was in a different world and often felt very alone.

I continued to focus on the mission. There was work to do. I knew the children were being loved and were well taken care of by their dad—with periodic help from my in-laws and my father. What else did I need to worry about? *Still...*

Kyle turned one halfway through this assignment. I was on the other side of the planet. Mothers typically spend a lot of time organizing and throwing grand parties for their one-year-olds. It's a monumental event in the lives of young families.

I didn't plan anything. I didn't do anything. I wasn't even with my child. I couldn't telephone home that day. I didn't want to think about all that I was missing. I kept telling myself I had chosen this life, this assignment. I also told myself the day would pass, and Kyle was so young he wouldn't even remember it. I buried deep in my soul my feelings of sadness, despair, and the certainty that I wasn't a very good mom.

It was a typical day for my team in the NIST. I had been reading through intelligence reports that had come in overnight, collating information and preparing a briefing to give to my commander a few hours later. I wondered where my analyst, Steve, and my communications officer, William, were as we usually started our day in the makeshift "office" together. In fact, I was a bit aggravated because I needed their input on the briefing, and they hadn't told me they would be late. I also knew there weren't many places they could be on the compound and so I assumed they both had decided to sleep in.

Suddenly, the noisy steel door of our small, sterile, cold CONEX box slammed open, and in walked my two partners singing a rousing chorus of "Happy Birthday." I was confused at first. My mind was focused on the documents in front of me. It wasn't my birthday. What were they doing? Only then did I see the single, sparkling candle firmly stuck in the middle of a small chocolate cake. I sat on the wooden bench that had been converted to an office chair and watched with astonishment as they smiled, laughed, and presented the cake to me with a flourish.

Before I could catch my breath or get out a word of appreciation, they began reciting aloud a poem they said they had written just for me, for just that day:

A Birthday Poem

Today's my birthday, Mom,
And you're far away.
But I know you're thinking of me,
On this very special day.
Although you're not here,
And that makes me sad,
All is not lost because,
I'm sharing it with Claire and Dad.

I know your job sometimes
Takes you far across the sea,
But fear not, I don't believe Daddy
When he says you've abandoned me!

You're not really missing much,
After all, I am only one.
I'll make a mess with the
Ice cream and cake, and Dad
Will get to clean up,
Now that will be fun!

You've got Steve and Scott,
The Major, Brian, and Rose.
And let's not forget Melvin and Woody,
Who by the way,
Had nothing to do with this prose.

So celebrate my birthday
With the Sarajevo gang,
And Mom don't fret
That you're not here,
Have a piece of birthday cake,
And wash it down with a beer!

I had been feeling tired, sad, and a bit lonely—in short, quite sorry for myself. This heartfelt gesture, though, filled me with gratitude. These people, whom I had only met a few months before, had gone out of their way to make the day special for me, even in this far away, scary, cold, unfamiliar place. These two colleagues had neither met Kyle, nor did they even know me very well. But they were there when I needed them most. I knew, too, that in this line of work I chose, we were like a family. A strange, different kind of family, but they were people I could count on who would hold me up when I was at my lowest.

I wanted to cry, to really cry. I thought about Kyle and what I was missing. I thought about what Kyle was missing. Then I thought about the kindness shown to me by these two newly found friends who I didn't even know a few months earlier. We were part of a military unit. It wasn't the place to show any emotion. I had a job to do. But, for those few minutes in my little corner of the container box that we called an office, I felt content and warm. I knew then and really believed that Kyle was perfectly fine celebrating his first birthday with his dad and sister back home. I also knew then that I would be okay. I had people with me who cared about what it really meant to be a mom.

Despite the distance from my two small kids, I was glad to be in Sarajevo at that moment. I felt that I was doing at least a small bit to help the people of Bosnia, as well as other mothers to one-year-olds and many more scared, starving children who were experiencing so much heartache and pain. I was only there for a few months without my family, yet the issues I handled, the things I saw, the people I met, and the history that was made during that time all profoundly and permanently affected me.

I returned to America four months later, but in Kyle's short world, it was a lifetime. He was walking, babbling, and had lots of memories from those four months that didn't include me. As I landed back at our small regional airport in the US, I couldn't wait for the expected, ecstatic reunion with my children. I walked off the plane and saw them waiting. Claire ran toward me with arms outstretched, but Kyle was reluctant. In truth, I barely recognized him. He had on an outfit I had never seen before, and he was standing upright on his own two feet. It was those few seconds that took my breath away. *Where is the baby I had left behind?* Only when he saw his sister in my arms did he finally realize he wanted to be part of the reunion too and smiled, a dimple forming on his chubby cheeks. I felt tears slip down my face and choked back sobs of joy and grief over what I had gained…and what I had lost.

CHAPTER NINE

WORKING THE ROOM

Around the World
1998-2011

I attended a lot of diplomatic functions, trying to find people with access to information of interest. For example, the plans and intentions of foreign governments, negotiation techniques, who was moving up and who was moving out of foreign government leadership positions, threats by certain governments or groups to our economy, personality details about foreign leaders, and any threats of terrorist attacks against the US. I was looking for nuggets of information that would help our policymakers make the right decisions.

It meant working all day—in the office writing reports, on the street looking for places to meet people, at events making new contacts, and trying to determine if I needed to meet them again. I would return home for a few hours in the evenings to make dinner for the family, help with homework or a school project, and then leave again, sometimes with Joe, to continue looking for contacts of interest at a diplomatic reception. Or I'd depart on my own to begin a long evening that included meeting one of my agents.

I liked attending events with my husband. I could work a room and cover a lot of ground in a short amount of time. I had to find the right people, initiate a conversation, determine if they were worth meeting again, and, if so, get the person to like me enough to *want* to meet me again, all within a few minutes.

I viewed a diplomatic function as work. Joe viewed it as an opportunity to meet new people. I had to assess everyone I met. I had to remember what I learned and from whom I learned it. Joe, in his gregarious manner, would also work the room, but he did it for fun and ended up with all kinds of new friends. When I needed a break for a few minutes, I'd look for Joe. He was always chatting and laughing in a group near the hors d'oeuvres table. I would gratefully stand with him while he talked and take a much-needed respite from being "on." I could relax during those brief moments, take a sip of water, and gather my thoughts. Rejuvenated, I would then leave his side to go find my next contact.

Joe knew the kinds of people I wanted to meet and would, for my benefit, make a conscientious effort to find those people during his walks around the room or even during his experiences out in town.

Not only did Joe work diplomatic receptions effectively, but he worked his contacts in his own jobs. He was my partner, and though he didn't know any of the specifics, as a smart, professional, interested American, he knew what I needed.

I often entertained at home over dinner or a casual lunch. It was so much more effective, more personal, and more fun. There is nothing better than sitting around a table chatting over a meal to get to really know someone and create a bond. Talking in our living room with drinks and appetizers in hand, then moving to the dining room table for a relaxed, casual dinner created a warm and friendly atmosphere.

People let their guard down in these situations. Making conversation was easy. This perfect setting, though, took time to prepare. These gatherings were not simply a quick stop-by of friends. They were work, and in my case, I did the prep *and* the elicitation. It took planning. I had to think about what I wanted to get out of the evening, what I wanted to say, what I didn't want to say, who would sit where, and what I would suggest for a follow-up meeting. All this before I even began planning the menu, shopping, and cooking. Most of the officers who entertained at home were men, and most of these men had spouses who didn't work outside the home. Their wives were often available and ready to shop, cook, serve, and entertain whenever necessary.

During these dinners, Joe was a great help in keeping the conversation moving. He knew how to let me focus on the individual with whom I was most interested while he chatted easily with the others.

As I gained seniority throughout my career, I entertained more often and on a bigger scale. We opened our house to all kinds of foreign diplomats, local host country officials, and State Department colleagues. They were often grand affairs—we hired a pianist to play our Bösendorfer grand piano, bartenders to serve the welcome drinks and work the open bar, assistants to decorate the house with lights and candles for holidays, and, of course, caterers to arrange a great array of finger foods.

During these official functions, the children were relegated to the playroom. They knew to keep a distance from the party scene. They were always well-behaved, respectful of guests when they did interact with them, and, most importantly, understood the importance of what I was doing. While we always included a few true friends on the guest list, most of the attendees were invited because we wanted them to be there for a specific purpose. I wanted to learn more about them and possibly develop a more personal relationship with them. I needed these guests to trust me and to feel comfortable with me, and I needed this time to get to know them better in a friendly, fun, and informal setting.

Women often perceive things differently than men. We pick up on nuances others miss. We more easily break through façades and can more quickly establish a bond. We focus on different characteristics, more emotional or intangible ones. Is our interlocutor happy? What are their goals, their aspirations? What are they doing to reach those goals? Do they even *have* any goals? What are their worries, their stresses?

At an intimate dinner at home with people seated in a strategic manner, I could quickly obtain answers to many of these questions. Answers we needed to move forward—or not—with a case. Answers that would tell me if I should arrange (or even have) that next meeting.

My job was not part-time. It wasn't even a full-time, forty-hours-a-week job. Rather, it was an all-encompassing 24/7 job. There was never a time I could say, "I'm not on duty," "I'm done for the day," or "It's not my job." There was never an opportunity NOT to answer the phone on a weekend. Signing up for this career meant it was going to be woven into every aspect of my life and it didn't take me long to realize, also the lives of my spouse and children.

During one of my assignments overseas, I was interested in a particular Romanian diplomat. He held a senior position in his Embassy and seemed to have access to information about his country's relationship with the European Union. This was something I wanted to know more about. He had two years left on his assignment and was in the country with his wife, three young boys, and a daughter. Initially, we met at a school event, and then our families began to socialize together. This was made all the easier because we each had a boy the same age, so playdates were convenient and looked natural to anyone seeing us together.

On one occasion, though, our rendezvous didn't go quite as planned. The diplomat brought his son, Henry, over to our house to play. I encouraged my son, Eric, to take his "new friend" for a walk up a nearby hill where they could do a little BB gun target practice. This would give me time to talk privately with the father. They left the house, and I settled in with my guest over a cup of tea to chat.

It seemed only minutes had passed, though, when I heard the boys noisily making their way up the outside stairs and through the back door. *Already?* I needed more time to talk to Henry's dad. I had wanted Eric to keep Henry busy.

Unfortunately, Henry didn't want to walk anywhere, and he certainly did not want to walk up a hill, nor did he have any interest in carrying or firing a BB gun. Eric tried to be his friend until both soon realized they weren't at all compatible.

Years later, upon my retirement, when I broke cover with my younger children and told them what I had been doing all those years overseas, Eric exasperatedly reminded me that he never did like hanging out with Henry and could never understand why I was always "forcing" playdates on him.

Now and then—not often, but once in a while—Joe and I did something just for fun, just for ourselves. During one assignment in a lively European city, every Tuesday evening for an entire year, we and two of our closest friends drove downtown to a tango class. This crazy, fun routine was just what we needed. By late afternoon on those Tuesdays, I could feel myself already starting to relax. At home, I quickly prepared an easy meal for six—our five children and our friends' son. Then, I carefully picked out a flowing outfit, pulled my hair up in a bun, and grabbed my tango shoes—a pair of sophisticated, sexy, handmade black and red dance shoes. Thirty minutes later, the four of us were sitting in a cute little Argentinian café in the heart of the city, drinking a glass of delicious red wine and snacking on a beautiful display of charcuterie and cheese. All this to get us in the mood for an hour-long tango lesson with two professional instructors, an Argentinian couple who moved with amazing passion and expression as they danced together. We laughed and drank and learned the delicate but powerful moves of tango.

There was little distinction between when my workday ended and when my family time began. Everything seemed interconnected. Perhaps that is why it all seemed to function so smoothly. I never shared what mommy did at work or who mommy met with, but I also never completely separated the two parts of my life. I was always thinking about what I had to do or where I had to go for work, and I was always thinking of what I had to do next for my family: a lunch was forgotten on the counter; the school nurse called with a sick child in her office; a parent-teacher conference was scheduled unexpectedly; we were out of milk; a birthday present was needed for a party THAT afternoon, and I had an agent meeting scheduled that same evening—a meeting that was pre-arranged and couldn't be changed or a diplomatic reception I had to attend to find a specific target I thought might be there. I had a report to finish writing and submit to our headquarters before close of business;

I had to prepare for a business trip the next day to meet with another target coming in from the Middle East; I had to arrange to have coffee with a developmental—someone I needed to get to know better.

Another time, I wanted a chance to get to know a particular Russian businessman whom I was pretty certain had close and personal ties to the Kremlin. I wanted to find out for myself exactly what kind of connections he had. Through various sources, I learned he would be attending a presentation being given at a think tank in the city. I crafted a reason to get a ticket to the same presentation, arrived early enough to watch for the Russian to enter the venue, and then maneuvered myself so I could sit near him. I didn't really listen to the forty-five-minute presentation about the agriculture initiatives in Northern Europe. I didn't really care about the topic. Rather, I spent the time looking over the room, watching the Russian's reaction to the talk, and mentally reviewing what I would say to him once I had the chance.

As the doors to the auditorium opened and people spilled out to the coffee bar, I spotted the Russian by himself at a high top. I approached, appearing to randomly choose his table to stand near.

"Interesting perspective on the European Union's role, don't you think?" I casually said, looking in the direction of the Russian.

"Hmmm…" he responded coolly.

I introduced myself. "I'm here on behalf of the American Embassy, and we are just beginning to try to learn more about this."

"Ah, the American Embassy," he repeated, adding with a coy smile, "You have a very large embassy."

I knew I probably wouldn't be able to match his knowledge of the presentation, so instead, I changed tactics and asked, "What office are you with, if I may ask?"

Without responding, he handed me his business card and glanced behind me as if he was looking for someone else or perhaps just wanted to appear as if he was waiting for someone. I wasn't concerned. Business card in hand, I now had a reason and mechanism to make a second meeting with him. We separated a few moments later and joined the others heading back into the auditorium. My afternoon had been successful.

I used these venues—a casual lunch, drinks at a café, a five-minute exchange between meeting presentations—quite often. It was sometimes all I needed to extract a date of birth so I could confirm someone's identity, obtain confirmation the diplomat had just spent the last year in the prime minister's office, or find out someone was returning to his home country the next day unexpectedly.

One of these persons of interest along the way was Louis. He was demure, and really quite shy. He seemed uncomfortable around people. He had a technical job at the state-run telephone company of the country we were in, a country at the crossroads of southern Europe. That's all I knew. He didn't seem to want to talk to anyone about anything. I wanted to get inside his head though. I thought perhaps I might get him to at least tell me what he did every day in his position. That would be a start. I wanted to find someone on the inside, someone who might be able to tell me who made decisions and who knew where calls were going and where they were coming from. If I knew that, then maybe I would be able to find the person who was making decisions for the radical oppositionists to the government.

The "bad guys" weren't using the country's telephone system, of course, but it was worth a chance to find someone who might know who the person in the radical group actually was. It was a long shot, but to me, it was worth the effort. More tries increased the chance for success. It was simple math.

I had Louis's name, and I knew where he worked. I planned and prepared for my next move. I created a script— what I would say, how Louis might respond, and then how I might keep him talking. I rehearsed in my mind what I wanted out of the interaction. I needed Louis to agree to meet me for coffee so we could chat more and I could begin to ingratiate myself with him.

It took four afternoons. On my third try, as Louis was leaving his building and walking to the taxi stand, I finally saw my opportunity. I approached him and feigned that I thought I knew him. He looked surprised and kept walking without saying a word. I wasn't discouraged. The next day, I tried again. This time, Louis stopped, probably because he was curious as to why someone would want to engage him in conversation. That was all I needed. After only a few minutes, I told him I didn't want to delay him, but could we meet for coffee the next morning. He agreed. It was a win.

Then there was Mohammed. I was on a mailing list for a speaker series. Every other month at a posh hotel downtown, a senior political or economic analyst provided their viewpoints about a current world issue. While the topics and subsequent panel discussions were interesting, more importantly, I knew I was likely to meet someone there who was plugged into their country's plans and intentions.

It took about six months, but I finally saw an opportunity. Mohammed, from a North African country, was new on the diplomatic circuit, and I found out through a bit of research that he was attending the series. Over the following months, as we regularly interacted before and after the sessions, I learned all about him—his family, his interests, where he served before, and where he wanted to go next. We talked about his work, what he liked about it, and what bothered him. Once I realized I was likely to see Mohammed at each session, before I left for the event, I prepared what I wanted to learn about him that day and what I was willing to tell him about myself in order to engender camaraderie between us.

He was smart, although a bit egotistical. Our conversations inevitably ended up with Mohammed "instructing" me about a particular issue or a particular part of the world. I let him pontificate. He needed to hear himself talk.

Mohammed knew the issues, and he knew where his country stood on those issues. It wasn't long before I discovered that Mohammed only liked to talk about what Mohammed felt was important. He had an ax to grind. He wasn't listened to by his peers or his superiors. I soon realized that because I listened to him, he was willing to meet me. After many coffees over many weeks—long after the speaker series ended—it became clear that Mohammed didn't care about what was really happening in the world. He didn't care about what was happening in his country, between his country and the rest of Africa, or between his country and the European Union. He had his own ideas, and to him, that was all that mattered.

My time was precious. I couldn't spend any more of it with Mohammed. I had other work that needed to be done. I stopped going to areas where I might run into Mohammed. There was only so much time each day, and I needed to make better use of mine.

In the early years of my career, during my assignment in Central Europe, I met Jean, an economist at a European Bank. His portfolio included several corporate mergers, but I learned after only one brief chat with him that he had several Russian clients. He was never, of course, willing to divulge who those clients were, but it meant he had access.

We met over lunch on several occasions. I invited him, his wife, and two young children to our home for a casual family dinner. Again, before each interaction, I planned what I wanted to learn from him. Sometimes, it was just another piece of his background, and sometimes we talked about his work and the important role he played in his bank. Even the venues I suggested as places to meet were thought out well ahead—it had to be someplace not too near his work, not too near his home, but not too far. I didn't want Jean's colleagues to wonder why he was meeting with an American. I didn't want them to wonder why he was periodically gone so long over lunch.

By the end of my time there, Jean considered me a friend. He had begun to provide information on what his clients were asking of him. He didn't name them—that was a line he wouldn't cross—but he gave me enough information to help us create what was happening between several of the key Western European countries and the economic decision-makers in the Russian government.

Meetings with my recruited agents took even more planning and preparation than the initial contacts with people I wanted to meet. When meeting fellow spies, our meetings and everything we discussed would be difficult, or at least awkward, to explain if we were stopped. These clandestine meetings could mean the loss of their livelihood, or worse, their lives. After all, these people were committing treason. It was my responsibility to keep them safe.

Wei trusted me from the start. We had become friends. After over a year of meetings and listening to her concerns and her wishes, I understood her. She felt safe with me. We initially met one day when our office facilitated a diplomatic social event. She was standing away from the main group of people, and I approached her and began some small talk. I eventually asked her to join me for lunch the following week, and she agreed. In French, over that first simple meal of noodles, we developed a bond—we were both women, both professionals in what was still a man's world, and both mothers.

The difference was that Wei still lived in a very oppressive society. In fact, even though she held a relatively senior position in her Embassy, and her husband, still back in their home country, held a senior-level job, she was always closely watched by her Embassy colleagues. In fact, they all watched each other.

Wei was rarely allowed out of her compound unaccompanied. I remember when our relationship changed from chatter about our daughters to planning a secret meeting. Wei was reluctant at first. It was risky for her to meet an American diplomat. Our countries were not friends.

"It's dangerous for me to leave the Embassy property. I cannot." She was insistent, speaking in perfect French. I again emphasized the importance of better understanding her country's new policies vis-à-vis the US and implored, "Can you break away for even just a few minutes during the obligatory exercise time in your compound's yard?"

"Possibly, but I don't know." Her dark brown eyes darted right and left. Her hesitation was palpable. She was scared.

I set a time and a place not far from her Embassy. A place she could walk to quickly but that wasn't on a busy street. I told her I would be there on Tuesday, then again on Friday and every Tuesday and Friday until she was able to break away. It worked. Most weeks, she was able to meet me, and we had a few minutes to talk about what she was doing in her work, what she thought I might want to know, and, of course, she always gave me news about her daughter, who was with her husband in their home country.

One day, Wei excitedly told me her daughter would be visiting. It was a long-awaited event as it was not usual that the children could accompany or visit a parent overseas. It was part of the control her government placed over their people.

"Let's plan an outing!" I excitedly suggested to Wei. "We can drive to the ruins outside of town, or take a boat excursion up the coast, or hike to the waterfall." I continued with a plan that was forming in my head. "I can meet you down at the pier, and we can drive from there. I'll plan the day."

I was ecstatic knowing this would give me almost an entire day to talk to Wei about her work and finally be able to really ask her details about some of the information she had provided—something our brief meetings on the street hadn't allowed. I would also be able to watch Wei's interactions with her daughter and discover even more about what was important to her. Also, I thought it was a way I could thank Wei for the risk she was taking in meeting me and providing me with intelligence on her country's activities. Her love for her daughter and wanting to show her daughter the country she lived and worked in but not being able to pull it together allowed me to step in and provide what she couldn't.

I took advantage of a delightful week of scenic drives and long walks to learn more about Wei and what made her willing

to meet me and divulge her government's secrets. Our relationship became stronger. Wei expressed her commitment to
working with me.

I continued to watch for changes in her personality, in
her willingness to meet me, and in her access to information
after the week's "vacation." We began to hold all our meetings
in cars. I picked her up, and as we drove out of the city, we
talked. Less time was spent on family and chitchat. Neither
one of us wanted to be seen in the vehicle together, so we
knew we had a lot to cover in a short amount of time. Wei
still trusted me. She knew I had important questions. She
knew I would pay her each time for the information, and she
knew that she could trust that I would keep her safe.

Every day, with every decision regarding my work, I had
to assess the risks—to my family…to the people I met along
the way…to my agents. Did risk mean loss of work for those
I met? Loss of life, perhaps?

I could have stayed in a comfortable, suburban,
American environment and probably eliminated most or
possibly all of these risks, but instead, I was on the street,
looking for people who would tell me the secrets their
governments were hiding. *What am I thinking? How much
risk am I willing to take? Am I really able to minimize the risk
enough to make this life manageable?*

While stationed in North Africa, I met another of my
agents who traveled in from a neighboring country. We met
regularly every two months. He often came to the country I
was in for his own business purposes, so the travel route was
natural for him. Tawfik was an older gentleman, debonair,
and tall, with salt-and-pepper hair, a kind face, and a big
smile. He was a senior official in his foreign ministry. He had
been working with us for a long time. Through a complicated

covert communications system, we arranged a place and time for each follow-up meeting. They were always held after dark and at places I had previously cased to make sure they were still viable spots. The location needed to be away from casual observers and easy to access and depart from. I would already know how to get to the spot, how to arrive without dragging surveillance, and how to safely leave the area. We rotated through four different sites so all I had to do was give Tawfik a number and he knew where to be.

It was close to 11 p.m. one evening. I had driven around for two hours already. I didn't have any surveillance. I was clean. I proceeded toward the meeting spot, a pull-off area on a small road reached after several turns. The area was encircled by tall pines, making the spot hard to see. Just before the last turn on the larger road, I stopped, ensuring I wasn't across from or next to any house. I had already turned the headlights off as I approached the spot. I opened the driver's door and retrieved the screwdriver from my pocket and an envelope from under my seat. Then, I knelt down near the front bumper. Within a few seconds, I had removed the diplomatic license plate and replaced it with a local plate. I then hurried to the back of the vehicle and repeated the same process. I quietly slipped back into the driver's seat, stashed the envelope with the plates I had just removed under my seat, put the car into drive, and eased around the corner. I continued forward about a dozen meters, then slowly maneuvered into the pull-off area where Tawfik waited in the shadows of a tree. He climbed into the passenger seat. I nodded at him as he settled in, and then I quickly drove away.

"Hello, Miss Ann," he said in his heavily accented English. "How are you this evening?"

Even though the preparation and planning for these meetings took so much time and caused my stress level to rise inexplicably high, I really did enjoy them. Despite the risks surrounding any clandestine encounter, it was just part of the job. Tawfik had been working for us for a long time. He knew what to do, how to act, what to say, and how not to waste time. And he followed instructions perfectly.

"Tawfik." I greeted him with a smile and then asked, "Did you have any difficulty coming here?"

"It was not so difficult this time," he replied. "This is a good spot. It was easy for me to take a taxi to the park and walk from there. I need to remind you, though, that last time was complicated. There were too many people along my route, too many people just standing around, and it didn't make sense then for me to be out walking."

I acknowledged his concerns and thanked him for the specifics. Tawfik was an excellent agent. He understood the business. He knew what was important.

I drove another half mile or so and pulled over. It was another place I had canvassed earlier. There were no cameras and no place a random passer-by could see us. Together, Tawfik and I sat in obscurity, talking about what he had learned at his office—things he knew I would want to know. We were there for less than fifteen minutes. Tawfik was intelligent and kind. I often thought how nice it would be to have a relaxing lunch with him and just chat about his background, his family, and his life. However, this was a clandestine relationship. We met in secret so Tawfik could pass me information that he knew would help the US in their relations with his government.

We spoke briefly about his current situation. Then, for the next ten minutes, Tawfik answered my questions regarding his government's activities in Africa. That is all we had time for. Tawfik needed to start his trek back to his friends so as not to be gone too long.

I turned back to the steering wheel and said, with a bit of urgency, "Tawfik, it's time to go." I drove a short distance and turned onto another dark road.

We nodded to each other, then Tawfik got out and went silently to his vehicle, never turning or waving or saying goodbye.

I continued a few more blocks, stopped my car, retrieved the original license plates from the envelope concealed under my seat, and remounted them. Then, I quickly returned the local plates to their hiding spot. I drove through the town for another forty-five minutes, eventually making my way home and crawling into bed just before 2 a.m.

Just another normal day.

Chapter Ten

Tip of the Continent

North Africa
1998-2000

In the air over Switzerland, heading to our next assignment in February 1998, there we were, four of us now and a third baby on the way. We landed in Zurich for a ninety-minute layover, then boarded a Swissair flight to continue the journey—this time to North Africa.

Landing in yet another foreign country far from home, for a brief moment, I had the same reservations I always had. *What am I thinking? What are we doing here?* Nonetheless, walking down the steps of the plane onto the tarmac, I looked around at the new and unusual scene, held tight to Claire's hand, turned to Joe, who held Kyle in one arm, and said with confidence, "Here we go!"

He smiled at me and, with no hesitation, nodded in agreement.

We were warmly welcomed by two colleagues who whisked us through passport control and began telling us how incredible the next two years would be.

We quickly became immersed in the rich, temperate Mediterranean climate with its sandy beaches and cloudless skies. We eventually stopped being surprised at the regular sight of camels along the roads outside of town and on the edge of the desert. We soaked in the explosion of colors on doors and windows in the neighborhoods, the detail in the mosaics on the mosques, and the ornate and intricate metal-crafted ironwork on the windows, all highlighting an exotic mix of Arab, European, and Mediterranean cultures.

Everywhere we went, we could sense the influence of the ancient Phoenicians and Romans mixed with the more modern feel of the Turks, the French, and the Berbers. We walked through archeological sites less than a mile from our house—ruins of water basins, stairwells, and aqueducts used centuries before.

As we drove along the edge of the desert through and around the country, we felt removed from everything— people, the world, civilization. There were few street signs to direct us. Instead, we paid attention to landmarks—an old building or a bush or someone's cow (hoping the cow would stay there), anything we could recognize as we made our way back north to the city.

Even along these desolate roads and into the sparsely populated towns, there were schoolchildren and parents, friends, workers—a whole community eating together in their kitchens, shopping for vegetables in the markets, going to work each day, meeting friends for coffee—just like in any other village or town or city anywhere in the world. We had been transplanted for a time to a new and different place, but in many ways, things were still very much the same.

We wandered into a small artisanal village known for its ceramics somewhat by chance. It was in the northern region of the country, about two hours from the capital city. We were driving slowly through a tiny neighborhood, looking for a place to buy a sandwich, when I saw it.

"Joe, stop here!" I said excitedly, certain I had found the recommended craftsman I had been looking for.

"Stop where?" he asked, seeing nothing but small, ramshackle structures.

I jumped out of the car and jogged towards an open garage door situated haphazardly behind some bushes. Inside, hunched over a crumbling workbench, was an elderly man with a weathered face surrounded by what seemed like thousands of ceramic plates and bowls. They were arrayed around his feet and hanging along each wall all the way up to the ceiling. This old, hidden-away garage was like an art gallery—an explosion of blue and white in delicately painted designs everywhere.

Through a combination of very broken Arabic and English, the skilled tradesman told us he had painted everything in front of us by hand, one by one. There were beautiful, decorative plates of all sizes and designs. I excitedly thought about these brilliant colors in my dining room and the conversations we'd have over the dishes. Gathering up a pile to purchase, I began to check each one for possible imperfections. After only a few minutes, though, I realized that it was the imperfections that made each piece so unique.

A long, sandy strip of beach lined with all-inclusive hotels on the northern coast of Africa was a popular weekend getaway for everyone working in the city. The area catered primarily to busloads of German tourists. Whenever we had a chance to take advantage of a change of scenery and found ourselves there, we experienced the heavy brown bread and apple pancakes made especially for the German clientele, along with the ubiquitous freshly squeezed orange juice and delicious, right-off-the-tree pomegranates.

A prominent hilltop town about twenty kilometers from the city center overlooked the Gulf that led out to the

Mediterranean. Houses in the characteristically Arab style with doors painted in striking geometric designs of blues, reds, and yellows and carved with detailed floral motifs lined the pedestrian-only streets. The white walls, blue shutters, and wrought iron grills provided a clean, picturesque, postcard-like backdrop as we meandered through the narrow streets, stopping at what soon became one of our favorite cafés that overlooked the sea.

In the southwestern part of the country in which we lived is an area known as the Gateway to the Desert, a place which grew out of a bed of red rocks. Following a massive flood in the middle of the twentieth century that wiped away the village, a smaller town sprung up and is today a welcomed oasis. It's also the site of an inviting, alluring, very authentic hotel. The town is surrounded by steep hills and wildland with clear water cascades and springs. We parked in front of the hotel, and before even unloading our bags, the children ran to climb the massive slope facing the hotel, finding rivulets and springs of fresh water along the way.

The desert surrounding us outside the little oasis was ominous, almost frightening. It was a landscape we had never experienced and one we didn't understand. As we explored, we found smaller, hidden oases and unique Berber villages with cratered earth shelters and troglodyte caves.

One day, driving through the rural countryside along roads bordered endlessly by olive trees, we rounded a bend, and looming in front of us was an almost completely intact colosseum. We piled out of the car and stood on a grassy knoll looking down into a massive sphere and the ruins of what we later learned was a significant Roman town dating from the second century. From a stone structure near the top of the colosseum, a landscape of olive groves and grassy fields spread out as far as the eye could see. As we drove and pointed out the uninterrupted rows to our kids, four-year-old Kyle confidently responded from the back of the car, "They aren't olive groves; they're just trees!" It was tough to argue, so I didn't even try.

As we continued to soak in the views of the countryside, a small truck came barreling around a turn from the opposite direction. The driver was a middle-aged man with a sun-beaten face. Wearing a white T-shirt and scruffy jeans, he was driving a small, decrepit moped and pulling an oversized, flatbed wagon loaded with hundreds and hundreds of cartons of eggs layered at least twenty feet high, all balancing effortlessly. Just another simple man doing his daily job in the middle of the countryside, oblivious to any encroachment of modern urbanization and seemingly unaffected by it all.

We wanted to explore the whole continent of Africa. It's an amazing, different world. In the end, we only saw a fraction of it, the most northern and the most southern tips.

I used our regular wanderings as an excuse to meet an agent at a resort on an island off the southeastern coast of the country. Our family excursion provided cover for the real reason I was there. During a previous meeting with this agent, I had arranged the whole scenario in excruciating detail. He would pass through the area for his own business purposes and stay at the hotel for one night. I would schedule a few days of vacation with my family at the same resort, a getaway from the busy city on a long weekend. We had prearranged a specific day and time to meet. Khalid knew exactly where to wait for me outside, a corner spot in the garden so I could pass him my room number.

On our second day at the resort, my family went to the beach for the afternoon. Joe knew I would find them when my meeting was over. Khalid arrived at my room at exactly the prearranged time. Our meeting lasted less than an hour, but it was all I needed. I was able to collect the additional information I had asked him for. He had the telephone numbers and the names of several people we wanted to monitor. To anyone else, it appeared each of us was there for a relaxing weekend. The resort's location and setup shielded us from random, casual passersby. The planned scenario worked perfectly.

We celebrated Kyle's fourth birthday just a few weeks after our arrival in the country. We were still living in temporary housing but wanted to try to make his day special, nonetheless. Just before leaving the US one month earlier, we had bought Kyle his first bicycle as a surprise (calling it the "crazy chicken"), but it was still in a shipment somewhere over the Atlantic Ocean, hopefully enroute to us. I was able, though, to find a small cake, some ice cream, and a few balloons at a corner market. It was enough—simple but festive.

Our life here meant that we all had to learn, understand, and appreciate the Muslim culture, including the meaning and importance of Ramadan. Between sunrise and sunset during the holy month, the Muslims fast. The pace of work and life slows down. I had to adjust my meeting schedules, the hours I was at the Embassy, and where and when we did things. When the Christmas season happened to fall during the same time as Ramadan, even less work took place. Ramadan became intertwined with our life. It determined who was working, when we could shop, and even what was available in the markets.

A few days before our first Eid, the feast or "Breaking of the Fast" that marks the end of Ramadan, we were relaxing at home when we heard chanting and shrieking coming from the street. We peered out across the fence encircling our garden and saw three men wielding huge knives walking up the hill toward our corner. Though initially a bit taken aback, within only a few minutes we realized they were simply advertising their "services." Upon request, they would slaughter your lamb and ready it for the big feast. A third of the meat from each household was traditionally kept by the family, a third was given to relatives, and a third was given to the poor. In town, stores had elaborate displays of new merchandise for gift-giving and bakeries sold loads of sugary, syrupy sweets. Families swarmed the streets shopping and preparing for the elaborate Eid meal.

Still in North Africa, I started my training for the upcoming Paris Marathon. I knew I could do it. I had been mentally preparing to run it for over a year. It was difficult finding the time as well as the motivation to train in this new country with so much to explore and more than a full schedule at work. And, by this time, I had three young children at home. Eric, our third, was born about a year earlier. I wanted to try a marathon, though. I loved running. I had always run, even during my pregnancies, often right up until giving birth. Still, this was different. This time, I was going to run twenty-six miles all at once, hopefully without stopping.

For months, I ran long routes on the dusty roads leading out of town. I didn't listen to music or use headphones. Instead, I spent the hours alone…just thinking. I needed the time alone. I needed the time to reflect.

I thought about all sorts of things. I made a mental list of all that I still had to do that day. I thought about where we might live next. I thought about how lucky I was to be able to run. I clocked my pace and ran farther. Occasionally, I felt that I was being a bit selfish. I just left everyone at home. I was taking time away from family activities when there wasn't a lot of time for that anyway. Nevertheless, running was therapeutic. I needed it.

The October weekend of the marathon was approaching. I felt good. I knew I would be ready. I knew I could do it. I had trained for months. My dad was going to fly to Paris from the US to support me and watch me run.

I planned to arrive in Paris on Friday, two days before the Sunday morning race. The week prior, as I did every Monday, I checked the secure, clandestine communication system we had in place to see if any of my agents had sent me a message. Because all our meetings were prearranged during a previous meeting, our agents only used this method if they had critical, time-sensitive information or had to change a meeting date or time. These messages were simply a backup to our face-to-face meetings.

That Monday, five days before I was to fly to Paris, there was a message from Ahmed, an agent I was handling. He wrote that he would be traveling into town unexpectedly over the coming weekend and needed to meet to discuss an administrative issue. This was an unscheduled meeting. By then, I had been meeting Ahmed for almost two years. He provided solid information, and I knew him well enough to decipher what he was trying to tell me in his messages. I was pretty sure I knew why he wanted to meet. He had been having difficulty with his secure comms laptop and it needed to be changed out. As always, we had already established a place for such a meeting, so logistics were simple.

However, this weekend wouldn't work for me. I was leaving Friday and flying to another country to run a marathon. I had trained for this for a year. It was a once-in-a-lifetime opportunity.

A colleague graciously agreed to handle the agent meeting for me. All was set. Then, I told my chief.

That didn't go well.

In no uncertain terms, he said it was *my* responsibility to meet the agent and that it was not negotiable. I panicked, even though in my heart, I knew he was right. This was not a job where I could pick and choose when I felt like working. I was responsible for my agents. I was responsible for meeting Ahmed. The job had to be done right, every time. *By me.* People's lives and livelihoods were at stake. I knew I couldn't let my personal activities get in the way of the mission. These were sacrifices I knew I might have to make when I signed up for this job.

But the marathon was something I had been planning to run for months. My mind had been focused on that goal for so long. As always, personal goals and work responsibilities were colliding. *Life wasn't fair.*

In the end, I rearranged schedules, flights, and lots of logistics. I made the meeting with Ahmed late Friday night, then flew to Paris the next day and ran the marathon on Sunday. I was less well-rested than I planned and a lot more stressed. Still, I ran the twenty-six-mile race in three hours and forty-seven minutes. My goal had been to finish running in under four hours. I did it.

This North African assignment had started for us like all the others. We didn't know anyone. We didn't know where to buy what we needed. I didn't know the route to work or even how to read the street signs.

Yet we'd made a go of it. We'd carried on and completed another chapter of our story.

Chapter Eleven

Out of Africa

North Africa
1998-2000

A few months into our North African assignment, we temporarily returned to the US to await baby Eric's arrival. Joe, Claire, Kyle, and I spent almost two months together—every hour of every day living out of a hotel—waiting for Eric John to be born. Then, on July 6, 1998, at 7:13 a.m., he arrived.

I was anxious. I didn't like not knowing what was happening in my office across the ocean. I wasn't comfortable wondering if the people I worked so hard to form relationships with were still meeting with the CIA in my absence. I was asking them to take risks. They were people who had become my responsibility.

My baby was about to be born, and I had two other toddlers to look after. Somehow, I had to get my mind around what was happening right at that moment in front of me.

I liked my obstetrician overseas. I liked the care I was getting. It was a familial kind of service, very personable. My doctor was also the person preparing the room and taking vitals. He was the receptionist taking calls and setting up appointments. He was the cashier taking the payments and, of course, the expert I trusted to make sure things were progressing as planned. He had been trained in France. He was calming and competent. I spent a lot of time asking him questions, practicing my French. I wanted to know his background and how he ended up where he did.

He had little experience with neonatal emergencies, however, and so, in an abundance of caution, I returned to the US to give birth. If extraordinary measures were needed, I wanted to be as close to home as possible. It was too dangerous to fly within six weeks of my due date, which meant I'd be away from the office for quite a while. It was a tradeoff. Ensuring my baby had the best chance of starting out meant adjusting my workload, my relationships, and my responsibilities in the office.

The cost for my children to fly back with me to the US was reimbursed by my office, though my husband's ticket was not. Those were the rules, antiquated as they were. But I needed Joe. Who decided that the father wasn't worth sending with the rest of the family? I needed him for emotional support and, of course, to help care for our other children while I was in the hospital. We had no extended family nearby that could step in.

Very early in the morning on July 6th, I had to get to the hospital. It was time. Our hotel room was not very big. Where were the car keys? They were always on the counter next to the refrigerator—except today. I had been through this routine before—gathering my overnight bag, planning my route to the hospital, and making sure the other children were accounted for—but now I started to panic. *Where were the keys?*

Every minute's delay made me more nervous and more anxious. I couldn't even walk anymore without pain shooting through my abdomen and down my legs. I sat on the chair near the door and watched as Joe dashed through our hotel's two rooms strewn with suitcases, stepping over toys and piles of clothes and papers, frantically searching for the car keys. After what seemed like an eternity, he found them—in the bottom of Claire's backpack! Did Claire not want Eric to arrive? Was it Claire's clever, passive-aggressive way of telling us something?

With not much time to spare and no time to question our precocious six-year-old daughter, I was at last on my way to the hospital. Then, not long after, I was holding our healthy baby boy, Eric. He weighed seven pounds fourteen ounces and was twenty-one inches long. A perfect little package. He was baptized a month later in the Upstate New York church I grew up in, the same church where I buried my mom, the same church where I was married. Life was carrying on in a seemingly never-ending circle.

Too soon it seemed, I was back to work in North Africa. Eric was only three months old. That first week at the office I had a business trip, but this time, thankfully, it only involved an easy plane ride to Europe.

Though the trip was just for one week, it was tough to leave the family so soon after being together every day for months. I wondered if Eric would remember who I was when I returned, if he even knew I was gone, or if he understood what was happening.

I had been through this before. I had experienced these same feelings with Kyle and with Claire. It was times like these, with three perfect children at home (one only an infant), faced with another trip I needed to take alone, when

I wondered if the job was worth it. These feelings weren't constant, but they occurred often enough. I'd wonder if the children really understood that I was leaving, that I wouldn't see them that evening, wouldn't have dinner with them, and wouldn't read them a story that night or the next. I wondered if they understood that I would always be back and they just needed to be patient.

As I left, Eric smiled up at me, his twinkling brown eyes melting my heart. It was as if he didn't have a care in the world. He really had no idea what was happening over the next few minutes, hours, or even days.

"Bon voyage, Mommy!" Claire bid me farewell with a big hug, using the French she knew. Kyle toddled over to me from the playroom and wrapped his little arms around my legs.

The trip was successful. I was busy, and the time passed quickly. It was good to be back home, though, and as I opened the front door, I smiled at the thought of sitting down to dinner that evening with Joe and the children. Claire talked about all the little French girls she was meeting at school. Kyle told me about his new friends at his preschool—Julia, the little Italian girl, and Ian, the little American boy. At the *maternelle*, located not far from downtown, the only languages Kyle heard all day from his teachers were French and Arabic, but he seemed to be adapting quite well.

It was back to normal.

Despite the family activities and the time I needed to spend at work or think about work, Joe and I still had to make sure Claire finished her homework on time and Kyle was ready for preschool every morning. Sometimes, getting it all done was a struggle. It was something I would deal with over and over for the next twenty years. I was usually very busy with work in the evenings. I often attended meetings that, for many reasons, could not be arranged during the day. So, the hours I was home with the children were precious to me. I had to be organized and focused.

Claire usually pulled out a book to read as soon as she got home from school. It seemed we always had to track her down and often found her curled up in a corner of her room engrossed in another chapter of a Beverly Cleary book. We would eventually convince her to put the book down and finish her homework while I prepared dinner and got the children and their backpacks ready for the next day.

Driving up and down the main highway from our home to Claire's school was precarious—unless it was the middle of the night and no one was out, which was rarely the case. The undisciplined drivers making crazy turns and the pedestrians trying to cross the road at random spots along the way made navigating the route scary. As I kept up with the ninety kilometers per hour traffic, people would suddenly appear on the side of the road, having come out of the bushes in the center median. They would take their lives in their own hands as they tried to quickly cross in front of speeding traffic.

Our neighborhood was just north of the city. It was a newer residential area with bright-white stucco houses. We lived up a hill on a corner as the road turned west. The marble floors throughout the interior gleamed and were slick. Eric learned to walk on these glistening but very hard, slippery floors. He fell so many times a day as he waddled from one room to the next that he always had bruises up and down his arms and legs and even, most noticeably, on his head.

Our house had a terrace that wrapped around the entire structure. A walkway meandered past lemon trees and green plants, up and down marble steps, and out past the front gate to the street.

Above a terraced garden left of the marble stairs leading to the front door was an outdoor patio covered by flowering vines. A turquoise, white, and sea-green tiled bench encircled the perimeter of the patio, and a magnificent, brilliant pink bougainvillea draped across the wooden beams, throwing its exotic flowers all over the tiled terrace.

The wife of the Deputy Chief of Mission (DCM) at the Embassy was a talented artist, and we commissioned her to paint this scene. We knew we wanted something to remember our time in this home. We wanted to cement in our minds the colors and the vitality, as well as the calmness and peace of our life during those two years. It turned out to be an exquisite piece of art that depicts the exact view we had from our kitchen window. She'd painted deep aqua for the sky, green tints for the trees, cream-colored shadows of the house, and the teal-colored bench. She perfectly depicted the steps that led up to the terrace, past the clay-potted plants to where the lush green trees and their twisted vines surround the seating area. The shock of deep fuchsia highlights the ever-present bougainvillea and provides that brilliant pop of color that we enjoyed every day.

During one of our adventures in the countryside, we found two gems in what would be considered by some to be a pile of junk—intricate, wrought iron window frames found buried in a heap in the backyard of a local artisan. We turned one of these inexpensive treasures into a coffee table and incorporated miniature tiles from around the region. The second window hangs on our living room wall as a piece of art. It stands as a framed reminder of the uniqueness of where we had lived.

The expansive area inside and outside our home was perfect for entertaining, and the children used the garden to play endless games of hide-and-seek in and around the plants, trees, and flowers. The entire outdoor area was watched over and meticulously cared for by Younis, our gardener, who wore a smile so big that his two perfect rows of teeth gleamed from far away. We initially thought hiring a gardener was quite a luxury. However, after one week of trying to maintain the plants under the sweltering Mediterranean sun, we were more than thankful he was there.

Younis didn't speak or understand a word of English, or barely French for that matter, so we never really knew if he had any idea what we were saying, and we never completely understood what he was saying. Still, he and Joe exchanged greetings every morning and laughed and joked with each other, almost like old school chums. Through a somewhat jumbled exchange one day, we learned from Younis, as he stood watering the periwinkle and snake plants that meandered down from our front deck, that his work was at a standstill. He explained, and we eventually understood, that he had to wait an undetermined number of days for the next delivery of fertilizer as the delivery method (via mule) was uncertain.

We loved seeing Younis every day with his sun-weathered face, dark eyes, and luminescent smile.

A security guard circled the premises several times a day to check on us and the house. The guards were supposed to alter their times so anyone wanting to know their routine would be thwarted, but we could never be certain they really did that. They were friendly, though, and even if they often helped themselves to the lemons and oranges from the trees in our garden, it was comforting to know they were nearby.

Strong, heavy metal grates covered the front door and first-floor windows of the house. Eric, who was now a spry and very active two-year-old, had a tendency to climb the grate, unhook the latch, hold onto the grates with his two tiny hands, and swing himself out. Once the swinging grate stopped, he would scurry down using the bars as ladder steps, then quickly scoot outside to the front garden.

One day—a day we are not proud of—we were all in the house. It was midmorning on a Saturday. I was in the basement doing laundry, and Joe was upstairs with Claire and Kyle when the doorbell rang. Joe looked out from the second-floor window and saw a woman carrying a baby standing outside our gate. Thinking it was a beggar and not wanting to let the woman into the garden, he ignored the incessant ringing. Eventually, out of frustration, Joe finally went out the front door, down the steps of the garden, and to the outer gate to ask the woman to move along.

Then he saw what he didn't notice from his view out the window. The woman was holding baby Eric! This time, after Eric had swung out on the front grate into the garden, he somehow kept climbing—right over the wall that led to the street. The old woman saw him leave our house and wander down the street. She knew where he belonged. She wasn't looking for money. She was simply an angel returning our child.

It was the eve of the new millennium, and we were still in North Africa. After lots of hype over what might happen to the world at the stroke of midnight on January 1st, 2000, we celebrated the long-awaited event at an almost all-night party at my boss's house. The venue in the northern part of the city had a spectacular view of the Mediterranean Sea in the distance. We stood on his terrace at the front of his house, gazing toward the glittering lights of the barges and other vessels reflecting off the bay.

We were overseas in what some might consider a "lesser developed" country. Would the infrastructure hold up?

Would the power grids stay functional? Would there be riots in the streets? Lots of important people had come up with theories about what we should prepare for, but we wanted to forget the worries and revel in all the good around us. We didn't know what would happen leading up to midnight or during the early morning hours of that first new day of the millennium. So, we just decided to spend the historic eve eating, drinking, and dancing with friends. The Y2K Community Bash pre-festivity checklist, sent ahead of time to all the guests, included:

1. Drop off money for spirits to include the requisite Millennium champagne

2. Drop off a favorite CD for the DJ to tape *(This was long before downloading music, iPhones, and Spotify!)*

3. Call if you need help getting to the party

4. Contact the organizer for potluck coordination ideas

5. Put kids in the car if you've got them

6. Fill up the gas tank

7. Unplug electrical items from sockets

8. Fill up the bathtub with water

9. Decide on which New Year's resolution to break

10. Say a prayer and come over and party with friends!

This North African assignment included lots of routine days with ordinary activities that have turned into good memories. We could have been anywhere in the world doing many of these same things. There were visits to amusement parks, birthday parties, playdates, family outings, shopping in the marketplace, walks around the old town with its twisting lanes and covered passages, and trips to the zoo. There were Easter egg hunts on the Ambassador's lawn and comparing notes about the best places to buy the freshest foods, stop for a coffee, or play in the park. There was teaching Kyle to swim at the small, outdoor Embassy pool and pushing Eric on the swings.

There are more unique memories too, like Claire experimenting with traditional henna tattoos and wearing her Hand of Fatima necklace, which is said to provide protection from the evil eye. There were excursions in the desert and foraging for food, trinkets, and toys at the outdoor markets.

Mass at the Cathedral in the heart of the city was in French. Attendance was sparse, in part because Catholics were very much still a minority in this Muslim country. Eventually, we began attending a small Catholic church located across a causeway from downtown, about twenty minutes from our home.

Kyle was more interested in blowing out the candles in the back of the nave and Claire was distracted by the ominous-looking statues up and down the main aisle. But one special day, among an eclectic assembly of English-speaking Africans, Filipinos and a smattering of Americans, Claire received the Sacraments of the Holy Eucharist and Reconciliation—her first Holy Communion. She had taken classes from the priest at this small church over several months and was the only one that Easter to receive the sacraments, making the event that much more special.

Life wasn't difficult, but it was certainly not convenient by Western standards. The simple task of shopping for groceries quickly became a long and drawn-out process. It required patience, timing, and flexibility. If we looked hard enough, we could eventually find most things that we needed. There were no glossy, gleaming, easily accessible stores. Instead, we had our little chicken shops, our little bread shops, and our little fruit and vegetable stands. Choices were limited to what was in season. There were lots and lots of oranges in December, for example, but little else.

For some, this was too much to handle, and so they shopped exclusively at the Embassy-run commissary. While the commissary had "essential" items like chocolate chips, maple syrup, or good American beef patties, choices there were limited, too, and prices were high. For our growing family, we headed to the local market every week instead to get the majority of our groceries.

I needed to set aside a whole morning or afternoon to shop. Everything took time. Our preferred local shop, with its open market stalls and small dry goods shop, was thankfully only a short drive from our house. Nothing there was prepackaged or even covered with plastic. People told me that meant "things were fresh." I became used to buying what was available, but I did often think about, and sometimes long for, the protected, greenhouse-grown heads of lettuce back home. Instead, I had to satisfy myself with a shriveled, moss-and-dirt-covered "fresh" pile of green leaves.

Beef wasn't always available, and when it was, the quality was questionable. The animal carcasses hanging from hooks made the walk between the beef stand and the chicken stand and all the way to the fruit and vegetable crates a bit precarious. The children and I would step around the splatters of blood dripping over our heads and slowly saunter to the fish section.

Chicken was a staple. Near the vegetable stand was the chicken stand. There were always a lot of chickens to choose from—all live and *very* fresh.

I had to get used to this routine, too. The young man selling the chickens took the bird I pointed to out of the cage. I listened to it squawk and shriek uncontrollably as the chicken man, with a cigarette dangling from his mouth, grabbed it around its two feet with one large, grimy hand. Then, he went behind a half wall and, suddenly, the squawking stopped. A few minutes later, the chicken man handed me a chicken—very dead, and thankfully with most of the feathers already removed. The man waited in the same spot, wearing his blood-splattered apron, as I fished out a handful of coins to pay him for our dinner.

Chapter Twelve

On Safari

South Africa
2000

In the spring of 2000, we took a three-week excursion through South Africa. Once we felt comfortable enough driving on the lefthand side of the road, we began our trek of the country in Johannesburg, then headed northeast, crisscrossing the Transvaal region and passing through the towns of Boksburg, Witbank, Middelburg, Belfast, Dullstroom, Lydenburg, and Hoedspruit. Finally, we arrived at Mohlabetsi Game Lodge, known as the "Place of Sweet Waters," on the outskirts of Kruger National Park.

We felt far away from civilization. It was a different part of the world than anything we had experienced before. It was so quiet. In the mornings, midafternoons, and even the early evenings, the only sounds outside our small, one-room shelter were the whispers of the trees, the caw-cawing of far-off birds, and the rustling of unidentified creatures moving in the bushes just outside the camp perimeter. We also heard the soft murmuring of the lodge employees walking through the camp and periodically the jeep drivers calling for their groups, but even these sounds were drowned out by the blanket of a pervasive, quiet calm.

We stayed in a family rondavel. It was comfortable, albeit spartan. Nonetheless, it had everything we needed—enough beds, lamps to read by in the evenings, chairs to sit in and rest our bodies after a full day in the field, clean toilet facilities, and space for the five of us to move around. Early each morning, we went on a game walk and, after dark, a nighttime game drive in an open Land Rover. Each outing was strategically designed by the lodge to allow us to feel a part of the surroundings, part of the reserve, and part of the habitat of the creatures that called the open land their home. It worked. We felt like we were witnessing, right in front of us, a magical experience.

During one of the game drives, we saw wildlife up close that we knew we might never see again in their own habitat. We came face to face with lions and elephants, two of the famous "Big Five" species considered the most dangerous on the African continent. We also saw so many zebra, giraffes, and springbok throughout our trip it almost became mundane!

When we came close to the giant animals, even Eric, as little as he was, knew to be silent. This was particularly important during the night game watches when the path in front of our Land Rover was completely dark, and we couldn't tell what was on either side of us or behind us. We were totally surrounded by the black night. We never knew what lay just around the corner. It was an awe-inspiring environment.

Clearly stated in the park brochure was the admonition, "You are entering the Kruger National Park at your own risk." We had been warned over and over by the park rangers, the employees of the Molhebetsi Lodge, and in all the pamphlets we were handed when we entered the park. We knew we could face danger if we were to leave the hard surface road when on our own driving through the park.

One late afternoon, just as the sun was setting, the warning became very real very quickly. We wanted to explore some of the park by ourselves. Of course, we planned to stay inside the car and on the paved roads. After only about twenty minutes of driving along a narrow, hard-surface road, winding through the quiet, in and around grasses and trees, and along small water sources, straight ahead and up the hill in front of us we suddenly saw the silhouette of something enormous. Joe slowed the car and we all peered through the windshield. Up ahead was a huge elephant, standing, it seemed, two stories tall and flanked by two graceful gazelles. We didn't move. We watched in amazement as the elephant's ears spread wider and wider and he began to stomp in place, slowly at first, then with increasing intensity. Off to the left of our car was another elephant leisurely grazing. As we looked out the windshield at the elephant on the hill in front of us, he suddenly began running, his gigantic ears flapping wildly. The huge animal looming before us seemed upset. He was getting ready to charge. We obviously had little previous experience with elephants, but our sense was that it would be best not to linger. I turned and looked at the children. Wanting to panic, I instead gathered my wits. I yelled for Joe to move the car. Joe yelled to me that we had to move the car. It was chaos. Claire tried to explain that she was sure the big elephant just wanted to visit his elephant friend who was calmly waiting in the grass.

After what seemed like ages but was really only a few seconds, Joe stepped on the clutch, put the car in reverse, then stepped on the gas and sped away in the direction from which we came. We looked back and, sure enough, saw the two huge creatures now peacefully standing together along the side of the road, not far from where we had stopped.

Even while frantic to get away, we both managed to shout at the kids to look at the big elephant. They were confused.

"Why are you yelling?" the kids shouted back. Then they added, "We can't see anything! You're driving too fast!"

A few days later, we left Kruger on a foggy morning and began our drive through the Transvaal. The narrow roads and hairpin turns through the mountains afforded spectacular views into the gorges and small, neat villages along the way, making us gasp at every bend. We stopped along the edge of Blyde River Canyon and looked into "God's Window." The cliffs dropped away below us into a lush gorge overflowing with dense trees toward what some consider to be the greenest canyon in the world.

We drove the Garden Route, more than 1600 kilometers along the southern seaboard of the country, heading to the must-see Cape Agulhas Lighthouse on the southernmost tip of Africa. We stood on a little piece of land, marked haphazardly by a wooden sign, and looked out at an invisible line where two immense oceans, the Atlantic and the Indian, come together. There, at the very tip of a continent, at the edge of two huge bodies of water, we felt insignificant, like tiny specks in this enormous world.

We spent an afternoon visiting the Cape of Good Hope Nature Reserve and the lighthouse at Cape Point, imagining magnificent vessels sailing hundreds of years ago between the two oceans. We had read that the Cape is also home to a huge family of chacma baboons, but it wasn't until we entered the parking area at the trailhead that we began to feel truly uneasy. The animals were the size of small people and were strolling around, making themselves very comfortable on the hoods of all the cars, including atop the minivan right next to ours.

After an hour of walking around the Cape preserve, we were safely back in our vehicle, all together and happy to get a much-needed snack and bottle of water. We began to slowly drive out of the preserve, navigating around tourists and, of course, baboons. Inching along the narrow road toward the exit of the park, one of the children yelled, "He's on the car!" The other two children screamed. A not-so-friendly-looking baboon had been chasing the car since we pulled out of our spot and was now climbing up the back bumper. Joe drove faster and tried to drown out Claire's shrieks of "Don't hurt him, Daddy!"

After what seemed like an eternity, we were rid of the baboon and away from his troop. That was when we turned around to check on the children and saw Claire with a sandwich. Suddenly, it dawned on us why the baboon had hung onto our car for so long. Claire confessed she decided to share a piece of her peanut butter and jelly sandwich with the baboon and had tossed it out the car window before we started to drive away.

As we left the small road and headed to the exit of the massive park, we passed an attendant with a stick whose only job seemed to be to keep the baboons off the cars. He was flailing his tool, but it had no effect as the animals seemed totally in charge.

Nelson Mandela was held in a tiny cell for eighteen of his twenty-seven years of imprisonment on Robben Island off the coast of Cape Town. As we visited this place, we tried to explain to eight-year-old Claire, four-year-old Kyle, and two-year-old Eric what happened in South Africa and why Mandela was such a hero. Though Mandela and his country's quest for democracy would be taught in their schools in the US, there was something about being in the exact spot where he suffered such indecency as a political prisoner, only to eventually become South Africa's first democratically elected president, that made us feel closer to the miracle. We knew the children could tell by our reaction that the place and the story held meaning, even if they didn't realize how much this one man had changed history. It was yet another time when our worldly experiences brought the past to life.

My father often said when asked why he chose to climb a mountain, swim a river, or run a hill race that it was because "it was there." So, for essentially that reason, we decided to climb Table Mountain. The flat-topped mountain overlooking Cape Town can be seen from far away, and its outline has become a symbol of the city.

Joe took Claire and Kyle and started their hike to the top. I stayed at the bottom of the path with baby Eric. I watched as the three of them began up a narrow, steep set of stairs that had been dug out of the side at the base. Then they were gone.

It wasn't long before my mind started to wander. Perhaps it was the usual worry of a mom with young kids. Maybe it was because I was used to being surrounded by more family members and suddenly it was just Eric and me. Perhaps it was the quiet of the natural environment that allowed uncomfortable thoughts to enter my mind. I imagined Claire and Kyle running away to see one of the mountain goats up close. I began to envision the three of them on the top of this enormous flat rock with nothing to protect them from simply peering over the edge then falling off.

What was happening to me? I wasn't afraid of heights, and it wasn't even me up on the top! I had these horrible and unrealistic visions of half my family just teetering off the edge of the mountain. I paced with Eric in the baby carrier, holding him close to my chest. My anxiety worsened. I paced some more. The time was dragging on. They had been up there for too long. I started to think about what I would do if…I had to make a plan. *Who can I call?*

Then, as quickly as my mind was racing, all three appeared at the bottom of the stone steps, laughing and out of breath. Full of pride in themselves, they turned around and gazed up in astonishment at what they had just accomplished. It wasn't until many years later that I told Joe about my panic-stricken anxiety as I waited for them below.

Chapter Thirteen

European Adventures

Europe
2001-2003

In 2001, we moved to Central Europe, where we lived in a spacious duplex with large windows, a fireplace, and enough bedrooms for everyone. Located within a group of similar-style embassy houses, it sat directly across the street from the international school where our kids spent their days. It was here, in a vibrant, lively, and cosmopolitan European city, that our fourth child, Alexis, was born. A few years later, this would also be where we'd have our fifth and final child, Katrina.

As we explored our new home, the neighborhood, and the city, we took long walks along the river that flowed just north of the downtown area. Wide, paved pathways on each bank beckoned pedestrians like us every day. People stayed into the late evening hours, dining and drinking on the barge cafés and in taverns along the way.

We wandered along the sidewalks bordering the grand boulevards that encircled the popular downtown area and hiked on trails through the parks that peppered the city.

There were opulent balls, world-renowned operas, staid diplomatic functions, trips to lush vineyards, and tastings of the local delicacies and their new wines. There were all types of art and music exhibitions. During wintertime, there were traditional Christmas markets with stalls selling gluhwein, wooden ornaments, and homemade cookies. There were visits to the pediatrician, teacher conferences, grocery store runs, children's birthday parties, and school performances to attend.

On Sundays, we attended Mass in a beautiful nineteenth-century, neo-Gothic style church downtown, then afterwards meandered across a big square to have lunch in the shadow of City Hall.

All very ordinary, everyday activities.

Our little white station wagon had served us so well during our North African tour. Suddenly, though, it was considered too old and rundown by the strict standards in Europe. It took a random person placing a hand-scrawled note on its windshield one day asking to buy it that led us to finally realize we should part ways. Still, it was bittersweet. We were emotionally attached to the rundown jalopy. It had taken us to some fascinating places.

Every school that the children attended overseas held "United Nations Days." All the children in the school showed off their own country's customs, food, and entertainment. African, East Asian, South Asian, and Central, Latin, and North American nations were all represented. To the children, while everyone came from a different place, at school and to each other, they were all the same.

I used the city's extensive but easy-to-navigate network of trams and trolleys to commute to work. I also used the trams, trolleys, and circuitous roads of the city for surveillance detection routes before and after meetings.

There were very long workdays during this assignment. I was out at functions looking for individuals worth contacting more regularly, I was planning an evening meet, I was coordinating logistics for an operational venue I had to travel to, or I was strategizing with my team on priorities for the week. During this three-year assignment, I was also pregnant twice. Alexis was born a few months after we arrived. And I was pregnant with Katrina during our last year there - a time when my workload was the busiest.

My route home from the office took about forty-five minutes. It began with a short walk to the tram and a handful of stops to the trolley line. I'd wait up to ten minutes at the corner where the tram and trolley intersected, then take a twenty-minute trolley ride up the hill to our neighborhood. After getting off the trolley, I had a ten-minute walk up a steep hill before turning left, then climbing steps that led to the common driveway of our townhouse development. It became tougher as my pregnancy with Katrina progressed, and even more difficult when I was carrying the groceries for the evening meal.

It was during those moments—and they came frequently—that I wondered why I was doing it all. Why did I have to work, grocery shop, make dinner, then do it all again the next day? And why did I have to do all that when pregnant? I found myself sometimes resenting Joe during those moments. He worked, too, of course. He didn't want to give up his career and I didn't expect him to. His colleagues appreciated and relied on his expertise. He had worked hard to get where he was and was good at what he did.

But he didn't seem to have as much on his plate—at least, I didn't think he did compared to me. Perhaps it was our growing family, the pressures of the job, or not having a plan for our future, but things were difficult. Life was stressful.

On the weekends when I wasn't working and I had a bit of a respite, we sometimes managed to travel to interesting places. For example, the lively and spirited city of Ljubljana, Slovenia, a city that attracted crowds of young people with its famous Dragon Bridge. Then we drove east and spent hours shopping for crystal in Rogaska Slatina, one hundred kilometers from the capital.

We lunched in Bratislava, Slovakia's capital on the Danube River. There, we felt all around us the confluence of Austrian, Hungarian and Slovak influences. We imagined Queen Maria Theresa of the Hapsburgs looking down at us from her castle windows.

We took easy, quick day trips to Budapest, the Hungarian capital. It was a city with all the comforts anyone could want and virtually no hint of the miserable, dull, gray communist days I witnessed as a student only a few decades before.

We visited Prague, the capital of the Czech Republic. As we crossed the Vltava River, Kyle and Eric dashed from one side to the other on the famous stone Charles Bridge, hiding behind the statues along the way.

We drove to Cesky Krumlov in the southern part of the country near the border with Austria, a place nestled inside a bend of the Vltava River and filled with medieval architecture.

We spent a week in Warsaw, then drove to Krakow, home of Pope John Paul II. The kids were not in as much awe as we were. To them, it was what they had grown up with—another café in another market square in another city in another country.

We spent plenty of time skiing. Garmisch-Partenkirchen in the Southern Alps has over seventy kilometers of slopes and quickly became a favorite spot of ours. It was here the children really learned to ski.

I skied while very pregnant with Alexis. She gave me even more reason to ski smartly so as not to fall. I was carrying precious cargo.

On March 14, 2001, at 10:44 p.m., Alexis Ann arrived…Alexis Ann, one of the alias names I had used in the past, and probably my favorite of them.

As usual, I wasn't ready. There were still things to do. I had meetings at the office that morning. We had a conference scheduled with Claire's teacher at 3:30 that afternoon. I had dinner to prepare. The list was endless. I had tried to plan for her arrival, but all my planning was useless. I never learned.

None of that mattered to Alexis, though. She was coming, and I had no choice but to let it happen. The city's maternity clinics were a true haven. Inside, they were calm and quiet. The nurses moved about softly and spoke in such soothing tones. It was a nice change of pace from maternity wards in the US, where often there is so much happening there is no time to reflect. I wanted to sit with my newborn, in the quiet, just the two of us.

It took some effort at first, but I made the conscious decision to enjoy my time with my new baby girl, to just be present with Alexis and take advantage of doing absolutely nothing for those first few days of her little life. I knew the opportunity wouldn't last long.

Once back at work, my days returned to the routine of feedings, bottles, and naps after I got home. We seemed to have newborns and toddlers in our house every moment of every day during this phase of our life. Most days seemed routine, but there were amazing moments too. Like the first time Alexis sat up or took her first step, and when she learned to negotiate stairs or uttered her first words. Watching the interaction between Alexis and her siblings, or just watching all these little personalities form, made each day unique and special.

We kept moving, kept doing things, kept exploring. Eric and Alexis were in a ski school for preschoolers while Kyle and Claire were in a German ski school. Within a few years, three-year-old Alexis donned her puffy pink snowsuit, moved up to the toddler-level ski school, learned how to put her feet in the bindings, and was able to jump onto the chairlift. She was ready to head to the slopes with the rest of us, take her place between our legs, and aim for the bottom.

We ascended the Zugspitze, Germany's highest mountain, via a cogwheel train. At the top, we looked down the mountain behind us and then to the front onto four different countries—Austria, Germany, Switzerland, and Italy. The glistening snow on the windswept face of the mountain so far up was stunning but made us grateful for our goggles. We started our descent far above the tree line but often stopped halfway down the longer, winding runs for a beer and a bowl of goulash. It was quiet so high up on those mountains. The air was fresh, and the exhilarating feeling through our bodies made us feel alive. Skiing became one of our favorite family pastimes.

Then there were the not-so-pleasant memories of this assignment. The times we questioned our parenting skills. The times we felt uncertain, lacked confidence, or were clearly out of our element.

Claire developed an infection in her leg. It began in her heel. We didn't panic…at least not right away. We often worried throughout the parenting years, but we rarely panicked. We also knew that the children periodically tended to exaggerate their symptoms and ailments. We told Claire to keep walking.

But her leg didn't improve. We were sure the issue would resolve itself. Eventually, though, she couldn't walk at all. That's when we decided it was probably time to call the pediatrician.

The house visits the doctors made, in these urgent situations, reassured us we were in the right place at the right time. We never learned how Claire's leg initially became infected, but once we were told how serious things were, we moved quickly. In fact, we patted ourselves on the back when we were also told that it was a good thing we called the doctor before she lost a leg! Claire started taking antibiotics and was told to stay in bed, to stay calm, and NOT try to walk. After two weeks, she was completely healed and back to dance class!

A few months later, another medical crisis presented itself, this time with Eric. Since cell phones weren't allowed in my office, I was unreachable at work. I felt confident or at least hoped that Joe would answer his phone if there was ever a need.

Our nanny at the time, Krystyna, was terrific with the kids and amazingly competent. She kept everything in the house in order, even teaching me how to eliminate deadheads from the flowers in our window boxes. When Joe's mom visited, I'd come home and find Krystyna and my mother-in-law at the kitchen table chatting about life. It warmed my heart to see two of my favorite people, each with such different lives and from different sides of the world, together in my kitchen sharing stories over a cup of coffee.

Krystyna could handle any emergency—until one day, she couldn't. Four-year-old Eric was in trouble. He was in pain but couldn't explain what was wrong. Krystyna telephoned our neighbor and friend, who also happened to be one of the nurses at the Embassy. Eric eventually calmed down, and the situation seemed to resolve itself. In an abundance of caution, though, we scheduled a pediatrician's appointment for the following day. Eric seemed back to his normal self by the evening, so we canceled the appointment. We were confident, sort of, that things had stabilized. It would have been complicated to get Eric to the doctor since both Joe and I had all day meetings. Anyway, Eric looked fine.

The "back to normal" only lasted a few days. Eric once again started writhing in pain. After many frantic calls, Krystyna eventually reached Joe at work. All Joe could hear was Eric screaming in the background. Now, we moved quickly. Within just a few hours, Eric was checked into our neighborhood clinic and prepped for surgery. He had an inguinal hernia.

How did we miss this? We had no idea how it had started or why it had manifested itself so quickly. Calls from outside my office at the Embassy had to be routed through a complicated mechanism, so our exact location was obfuscated. As soon as Joe was able to reach me, I ran out of the office and hopped on the first tram I could find that went straight to the clinic.

Eric was put under anesthesia. It took only thirty seconds for him to be completely unconscious once he was injected with the drug. We hadn't had any time to check reviews on the hospital, the surgeon, or the staff. We felt helpless as we watched Eric fall into a deep, deep sleep, then quickly be wheeled away.

The surgery worked. Eric recovered quickly and was back to his carefree self only a week later. The incident only reinforced for us the notion that, in the end, we often really have very little control over things.

We did take time to reflect that every time something happened to one of the children, we had to learn to stop, take a deep breath, then rethink our plan.

We had to adjust.

Then, Kyle was sick. Miserable, really. It didn't take long for our pediatrician to diagnose a severe case of tonsillitis.

Within two days, Kyle was admitted to the hospital to have his tonsils removed. While this kind of surgery might be considered simple, we were now adding into the mix a foreign hospital, non-English speaking medical personnel, exams, and warnings and paperwork all in a foreign language. Nothing was easy.

It was early June 2003, and a beautiful sunny afternoon. I picked up Claire and a few of her friends at school, then drove them to a local swimming pool. I was very pregnant with Katrina but felt fine. The girls threw their towels on a lounge chair and jumped into the deep end. I waddled a few steps behind and once I eventually caught up, slowly lowered myself onto the pile of towels which provided me with some nice cushioning over the thin, plastic lounger. It wasn't long, though, before quick, successive pains interrupted my power nap. The pressure in my midsection increased, and I started to double over. I looked up and caught a glimpse of the children laughing as they swatted a plastic ball back and forth. I sat still as long as I could, hoping the pain would subside.

The contractions were intermittent at first. I had just seen my doctor that afternoon. She told me that once the contractions started, everything could happen quickly with this fifth baby. However, I wanted to let the girls play, to get through the afternoon, then get them all home safely.

What I wanted and needed were two different things. I couldn't wait any longer. I weakly called out to Claire to get her friends. I gathered their towels. Then, with me leaning on the girls, we slowly made our way to the car. Once in the driver's seat and knowing I was headed in the right direction, I felt a bit more at ease. At least I was somewhat in control. I managed to drop Claire's friends off at their homes then drove quickly to our house and announced to Joe that it was time to get to the hospital.

I didn't leave myself much time to spare. Katrina was born just an hour after I arrived at the clinic that evening. I was back in the same spot where Alexis was born two years before. Once horizontal and in the care of the nurses, I was relieved. I felt confident this experience would be as pleasant, wonderful, warm, and inviting as it had been the first time I was there.

Only six weeks after Katrina was born, we were on the road again. My next assignment was back in America.

The moving company arrived at the house, and in a controlled whirlwind, workers wrapped, packaged, boxed, and rolled all our belongings, leaving only a few things we would ship by air and some clothes to carry in our suitcases.

I was deeply grateful to my mother-in-law for coming to stay with us during this crazy period. We weren't set up to entertain, play tourist, or even be very good hosts, but she didn't care. She was there to keep her angel eyes over Katrina. The two of them stayed ensconced in the guest room on the first floor of our house while Joe and I negotiated around the movers. Things were stressful and fast-paced, but every couple of hours, I would sneak off into my mother-in-law's room, sit with her in the quiet, feed Katrina, and relax. Katrina was safe and content. That room was my refuge.

Chapter Fourteen

On the Street

Around the World
1998-2011

I often think about the irony of my work. We strived to raise our children with the proper morals, to know right from wrong, and to always tell the truth. Yet, my profession required that I lie when necessary. I had to be able to lie with confidence and conviction, to be deceptive, to skirt the truth. I also had to know *when* it was acceptable to lie and be able to understand when it was entirely wrong to do so. As with everything, I had to walk the line carefully. It takes a certain kind of person to be able to quickly adjust their way of thinking and pivot when necessary.

I hid what I did for a living. I never talked about my workdays, about the places I went or the people I met. I didn't like to talk about myself really at all. I wanted to keep a low profile. Even the children didn't ask about my days in the "office." To them, I was just "at work." They had other things to think about anyway, things important to them—friends, sports practice, school projects, weekends.

CIA officers lie to protect those we ask to work for us. We lie to protect our colleagues, our families, the mission and ourselves. Yet, within our relationships with colleagues and families, we must be truthful and transparent. It is important to instill integrity and honesty in our children even though at times, for their safety, we may have to omit certain things or stretch the truth.

This dichotomy can be complicated. It can cause self-doubt and severe self-analysis. It can disrupt families and cause dissension and divisiveness. In the end, it's a balance—not an impossible one to find, but critical to understand.

The art of getting people to talk about themselves and what they do without giving anything up about yourself can be tricky. Some consider it a talent. It takes practice to perfect the skill. If you want information, I firmly believe you must go get it. Engage with people, pursue them, be persistent, and use your imagination. Cull for details, establish a bond. Make the person feel comfortable. Make the person want to talk to you. Drop details about yourself if necessary—but only fragments, nothing more.

Looking for clandestine meeting sites and finding circuitous ways to get to those spots was something I did every time I left the house or office. From the moment I landed in a new city, I had to learn everything about it. I had to find the perfect setting for a meeting—quiet but not too quiet, easy to get to but not too easy to find. I had to look for places to stop to see if anyone was following me. I had to create casual-looking reasons to drive a certain route.

My life as a mom and my life as an operations officer intersected every day. I often looked for the locations or routes I needed when I was driving Claire to her weekly dance class, or when the children and I went to a museum on a weekend, or when I was dropping off payment at the pediatrician's office, or when I was picking up one of the children's friends for a playdate. I looked for that perfect underpass, the unobtrusive corner, the out-of-the-way alley or covered shopping atrium. These were places where I knew I could conduct a "brush pass" or a "brief encounter" to quickly hand off information or a piece of paper. I looked for spots I knew would be out-of-the-way enough to safely pick up an agent in my vehicle.

Timing was critical—getting the children to the school bus before it pulled away from the curb, meeting an agent at a prearranged site, arriving at the train station or airport on time, and making the phone call to the nanny when our plans changed. What would happen if a train was delayed, our car broke down, there was a traffic accident, the restaurant for the meeting was closed, there was an unexpected knock on the door, someone stepped in my way, or questions about my passport at the border took too long?

I had to expect the unexpected.

The day before I was to meet a sensitive agent in a small European country, I was at a car rental office. I was right on time, just as I had carefully planned. I was going to pick up an easy-to-maneuver vehicle and continue my journey to a small, somewhat sleepy town about eighty kilometers west across the border in a neighboring country. The employee behind the counter asked politely for a second piece of identification, something with my address.

Instantly, everything became complicated. I didn't have a second piece of identification. I was traveling undercover, in an alias, and only had what I was given—a passport and an international driver's license.

It was such a simple question, but it changed everything for the next few minutes. I had been calm. Things were going well up until that point, but now I suddenly had to think very quickly. I didn't have a permanent brick-and-mortar address. The address on my license wasn't real. I had nothing else to show.

I took a deep breath and began.

"I'm sorry," I said with more confidence than I felt. "I started out this morning from Belgium," I lied. "I only have my driver's license with me. I didn't want to travel with all my documents and risk losing something."

"How long have you lived at this address?" the rental car employee asked, pointing to the post office box address listed on my license.

I saw what he was trying to do. "Oh, that's just where I get my mail," I explained. "I live in the city. I'm so sorry to make things difficult for you." I apologized again.

With a bit of an exasperated look, the twenty-something employee looked down at his paperwork, then pushed a button on his computer and printed a contract. He asked me to sign at the bottom then handed me a set of keys.

With great relief, I smiled, thanked the young man again, turned around, and quickly exited through the door toward the parking lot.

I didn't panic. I didn't give up. I created a story on the spot, then confidently continued with my plan.

I was handling an asset in Northern Europe, meeting him regularly every two months. My trip required crossing several international borders. Each time I traveled to meet this person, I changed my route slightly, and I always switched up the days and times I left my starting point.

I departed one city by train and arrived in a second city by bus. There, I planned to meet someone who would give me a new set of documents substantiating a new identity. I proceeded to the designated meeting spot near a wooded area of a large park. Within a few seconds of my arrival, I spotted my contact across the park between two buildings. We crossed each other's paths for a brief moment. I handed him my true-identity documents and received from him my alias set. Now, I was ready to continue my travels under a different name and with a different background. This would allow me to meet my asset without creating any connection between him and a US diplomat. I was familiar with the documents in the envelope handed to me. I had studied them months earlier and had memorized the details.

The package included a driver's license, a passport, a credit card, a library card, and some miscellaneous discount cards from several different stores. In only a few minutes, I had a whole new identity. I was ready. I knew I had to be prepared to respond if someone called me by the new name or if I was questioned about my new persona. Following the document exchange, I continued to my agent meeting via a second train to a third city.

As long as I felt things were going as planned, I kept moving. Finally reaching the exact place I wanted to be, a quiet corner on the south side of the canal in the northwest part of the city, I saw my agent waiting ahead about twenty-five meters, just slightly inside the tree line. This was the exact spot we had planned a few months before.

I breathed a sigh of relief. Not only did we both make it to the site successfully and at the precise time, but we were both safe. Every minute leading up to the meeting had been meticulously executed. When it worked, it was amazing.

If someone sat next to me on a plane or on a train and asked what I did for a living, where I was from, or where I was going, I would smile, nod, give a one or two-word response, then politely put on my headphones and open a book. That is, unless I was interested in talking to the person because they might have access to intriguing information.

If I was interested in starting up a conversation with someone in particular, one or two questions were all it took to get the person talking incessantly about family, vacations, or hometown. This was how it always went.

Whether I was in a friendly city or a hostile one, whether I was surrounded by people or on my own, whether I understood the language and the culture or was in a place for the first time, there was always some risk. Yet, I couldn't assume everyone was out to get me, either. I was aware of my surroundings, where I was and who was near me. I didn't want to become complacent or rationalize away the odd question or the seemingly periodic anomaly. So much depended on knowing if something just didn't feel right. I had to have a story for wherever I was and whatever I was doing. Why was I out so late? Why was I going in that direction? Why was I at a particular place to begin with?

One of my contacts I was scheduled to call on a specific evening didn't know I worked for the US government. Instead, I had created a story that allowed her to think I worked for a private company and wanted her to "consult" on some important issues for me.

I left my house at about 7 p.m. and walked a very indirect route to a phone booth I had scoped out the week before that was off the beaten path. There, I dialed her number from memory. I had called her on that number before, so I knew it worked. I planned on having a short call just to confirm the meeting we had arranged the previous month.

This time, though, something didn't seem right. Instead of hearing a voice I recognized, a man answered, and when I asked to speak to Layla, he quickly said she wasn't there.

Without waiting for me to ask anything more, he added that she would no longer be available.

I was frustrated. It had taken me several hours to reach the spot to make the phone call. I was annoyed at first, then concerned. I tried to imagine what might have happened for her not to be there. She was always available in the evenings. I was worried. I didn't expect someone else to answer the phone. My contact did not know who I really worked for, so the situation was more complicated. Someone knew she shouldn't be speaking with me. I knew, right then, that it was safer for me *and* for my contact if I just walked away from the situation.

It was unfortunate. I had spent a lot of time working this case to get to the point where it was reaping benefits. As difficult as it was, though, I knew abandoning it quickly was the right decision.

CHAPTER FIFTEEN

EGYPTIAN NOMADS

Egypt
1999-2002, 2009

The first time we visited Egypt, Eric was just a toddler. The Egyptian Museum is housed in a massive, majestic, neoclassical, pink sandstone building in the center of Cairo. It is the oldest archeological museum in the Middle East and is packed full of ancient treasures. An entire floor of this famous museum is dedicated to the Royal Mummy Room. Eric stood his ground outside the large doors leading to this enticing space. He was not going in. He had no interest in the Mummy Room. He was just too scared. Kyle and Claire chided him, trying to coax him along. Joe and I chuckled at his protestations.

Before long, Eric realized he had no choice. He imagined having to endure the joking of his siblings forever. He also didn't want to be left behind looking at what he thought were just random pieces of stone. So, we all proceeded in.

The real-life relics were ominous, dramatic, and yes, a bit scary. The newly renovated Mummy Room had opened in 1995, several years prior. The bodies of Egypt's most illustrious kings and queens, once very much alive and ruling Egypt, were all there—Ramses II, Seti I, Tuthmosis II, and Queen Meret Amun. Inside the room, it was somber, as if inviting us all to join them in their peaceful afterlife.

After the museum, we took a harrowing van ride through the chaotic streets of Cairo, then continued west to the outskirts of the city and stopped at the Great Pyramid of Giza. While the Pyramids had already become commercialized as a top tourist site, we still stood in awe of these great shapes. Their immense presence, their historical significance, and the mystery that surrounded their creation filled us with amazement. When standing directly in their shadow, the Pyramids created a surreal feeling. How could these structures, built so long ago, still be standing today and look almost exactly as they did three thousand years ago?

We knew it was likely that in the not-too-distant future, the modern-day elements in the area, such as the bright, gaudy neon signs, the bustling Pizza Hut and KFC chain restaurants, the merchants selling plastic souvenirs, and the trucks delivering fruits and vegetables to the outdoor market would all change or even disappear—yet the Pyramids at Giza, the very same pyramids we were looking at that day, would still be standing.

After traveling around the base of the Pyramids on camels and exploring the Sphinx, as a treat for the kids, we went into the Pizza Hut that was positioned facing the huge stone wonders. We ordered a large cheese pizza, knowing exactly what we were going to get from this very American restaurant while we sat looking out the window at the ancient Pyramids. It was such a contradiction, a testament to the ephemeral *and* the permanence of things, the existence of both together, right in front of us in the same view.

We finished our pizza and walked outside into the hot, desert sun glinting off the limestone Sphinx looming before us.

We walked maybe fifteen paces when a young Egyptian man whom we had seen behind the counter in the Pizza Hut came barreling out the door running towards us, waving frantically. In broken English, we understood he was saying, "Your boy, your boy!" as he pointed to a cute, little, blond-haired child still sitting inside the restaurant with his head on the table, eyes closed, fast asleep. A second later, we recognized it was Eric!

Apparently, he had decided to take a nap in the shadow of the Great Pyramids after his filling meal, and somehow, we had headed right out the door without realizing we had left him behind!

Later that same week, we meandered down the mysterious yet unspoiled Nile River, floating from the Corniche just north of our hotel for several kilometers on "feluccas," ancient broad sailboats. Along the way were views of both crumbling stone buildings and modern, high-rise hotels.

Downtown was noisy and crowded, with cars racing in a dozen different directions. Small statues of Anubis, the god of cemeteries and embalming, portrayed as a man with a canine head, were seen in every gift shop on every corner. We walked through Islamic Cairo then the Garden City to the Cairo Gates, through the Khan El-Khalili souk and Coptic Cairo, the center of Egyptian Christianity for the last two thousand years.

It was a scorching hot day when we visited Luxor, the Valley of the Kings, and the Valley of the Queens. Massive Karnak temples decorated with statues of Ramses and his spouse, Nefertiti, stood tall near the bank of the Nile. Walking through the ancient Luxor Temple and around the colossus of Memnon and Nefertiti's tomb in the Valley of the Queens made us feel truly insignificant.

In the Valley of the Kings, we moved along past one stone entrance after another that led down to tombs deep underground. The searing heat became almost overwhelming. The sand blew, and it was desperately arid. As we walked along the worn, dusty path following so many tourists who had gone before us, we kept thinking of those buried beneath. So much history, a whole civilization.

The heat bore down on us. We heard a weak cry, turned around, and saw Claire looking very pale. It was only a matter of time. She wobbled a bit, and before we could get to her, she vomited all over the Royal Road. We prodded her to continue despite the heat and her upset stomach. These tombs and all that surrounded us were the kind of thing one might only see once in a lifetime. We couldn't stop the visit because of a bit of nausea!

In the end, we took a break and let Claire sit in the shade to drink water and cool down. The people working at the site said her reaction wasn't unusual, as the heat can often be oppressive. After a few minutes, with Claire feeling better, we continued along the path.

These excursions to Egypt never disappointed. They were filled with astounding culture, blue skies, incredible history, sun-drenched beaches, fascinating people, stunning mosques, exquisite museums, and so much more.

Before leaving the hotel on the last day of one of our several visits to Sharm el-Sheik, a coastal town on the Red Sea, a few years before our youngest, Katrina, was born, I wanted a picture of our four children. I lined them up in a row in front of a stunning bougainvillea hanging over the balcony outside our hotel room. The bright blue sea glistened brilliantly in the background—a perfect setting for my four adorable children.

Things started to quickly unravel when Alexis insisted on seeing the picture on the digital camera each time I clicked. Then she wouldn't smile, then she wouldn't stand near Eric, then she wanted her pacifier. She became hysterical, pulled away from the others, and cried and fussed incessantly. We got a picture, and the picture says it all— three smiling children all looking directly at the camera and one child, off to the side, eyes squeezed shut, her face in a tight grimace.

On a separate trip to Egypt, we lost an entire suitcase somewhere between the airport in Cairo and when we landed back home. Foolishly, we had put our video camera full of priceless memories in the suitcase, which probably made it a prime target for theft. What was far worse than losing the video camera, however, was losing Sheepy, Eric's beloved stuffed animal. It was a long grieving process for Eric until we eventually acquired Sheepy's "cousin," though, in truth, Eric was never completely satisfied with the pseudo-replacement.

There's one particular Egyptian memory we could never capture with a camera. I was a few months pregnant on that trip with our fifth child, and on a warm, sandy beach in Sharm el-Sheikh, we named her Katrina Elise. Joe had always liked the name Katrina and I had always wanted the name Elise somewhere, somehow. So, we compromised. It was a special time. We were in a beautiful place. Life was treating us well. We had a lively, growing family, and we were going to add one more to the mix. We knew, then, that our family would soon be complete.

Chapter Sixteen

9/11 Attacks

Central Europe
2001

It was September 2001, and I was a mom to four little kids. In the office, I was in charge of a group of people focused on finding targets who had information about the impending war in Iraq. It was a difficult task, but we were making progress. We had a plan. I had created a comprehensive picture of potential targets in the region, and we knew how we were systematically going to try to find them. Every day at home, I was also making sure my growing family had what they needed.

Then, everything changed.

I kept a journal for each of my children after they were born, at least for their first several years. Here are excerpts from some of those pages.

Journal Entry – 26 September 2001: *Claire—a terrible, terrible tragedy took place a few weeks ago in the United States. I've often thought that I should write more about the times, world events, and that sort of thing, but I never do—it's all I can* *muster to put a few thoughts down once in a while, but what happened is unprecedented and hopefully will never, never, happen again. On September 11, 2001, people's lives changed forever. A plane was hijacked and flown into one of the World Trade Center buildings. Eighteen minutes later, a second hijacked plane was flown into the second World Trade Tower. Then, a third hijacked plane crashed into the Pentagon in Washington, and, finally, a fourth crashed in a field in Pennsylvania, also hijacked.*

You're old enough, Claire, that you may remember this. Images of the planes flying directly into the Twin Towers were shown over and over again on the news. About two hundred people were killed at the Pentagon, including those on the airplane—and over six thousand are missing and presumed dead at the World Trade Center site. Six thousand! The number of people affected by each death and, thus, the number touched by this tragedy is enormous! Osama bin Laden is considered to be behind the attacks, and right now, the country is planning retaliatory strategies. In the meantime, though, the US has rallied together, flags fly everywhere, and the American spirit is very much alive.

Since we're in Europe, though, we are keeping a bit of a low profile. Sometimes, it makes me feel removed from the tragedy a bit, but it's more important to not stand out as a target. For you, Claire, I hope you never have to experience such tragedy up close. I hope you're never left alone like many of the children whose parents were killed, and I hope you grow up learning that there are many, many more wonderful things in the world than there are tragedies.

Journal Entry - 10 December 2001: *The United States is still reeling from the terrorist attacks against the World Trade Center and the Pentagon. It's really incredible—about five thousand people were killed, and it plunged the country into war. We've been bombarding Afghanistan for two months and looking for Osama bin Laden, the perpetrator of the attacks in the caves of Afghanistan. Claire—it's the country's primary focus. There's been a lot of fallout, everything from the cancellation of the school's Halloween party to much less air travel throughout the world. It has changed people forever, in part making people appreciate what they have and realizing no one is one hundred percent safe.*

Once we took stock of what had occurred and realized we had a job to do, the intensity and direction of our work in the CIA increased a hundredfold. I devoted even more time to the mission. The most important thing at that moment was to find out who had committed this unspeakable terrorist act against the US and why. At the same time, though, I had to ensure my kids, all still very young, were safe and at least understood to some degree what was going on around them, what had just happened in the US, and what we were trying to do to make sure it never happened again.

Within days of the attacks on the Twin Towers, the entrance to the children's international school was flanked by soldiers holding AK47s and accompanied by trained attack dogs. They stayed at the doors from that day throughout the remainder of our time in that city.

While we watched the news of how Americans in the US were rallying, waving flags in the street and pulling together as a nation in defiance of what had happened, all of us working overseas were told to keep a low profile, to not fly the US flag, and to be discreet as we moved around the city. Extra guards were placed outside the US Embassy. No one knew if there would be another attack or who the next target might be.

Everyone was on edge. It was a complete change to our day-to-day life and one we sadly had to get used to. The situation created a different vocabulary at work—and at home. We had never discussed the subject of terrorism with the children. We had never created terrorism as a Priority One target across our work portfolios.

Every person of my generation, and certainly everyone who worked at the CIA during this period, remembers exactly where they were, what they were doing, and how they reacted to the events of 9/11. For me, it was midafternoon. I had been in this Central European country only about one year. I was at my desk in the Embassy when, all of a sudden, I heard a commotion in the center of our office space. I saw people running toward the conference room. My instincts sharpened. I followed them, sensing danger.

People were crammed around the conference table. The television, hanging from the corner of the room's ceiling, was on and set at a high volume. It was tuned to one of the local news stations. A frantic-looking announcer was shouting into the camera. Scenes of New York City loomed on the screen. Then, there was a shot of the Twin Towers. I didn't understand what I was watching. All I saw on the television was chaos, people running and screaming. As I began to slowly realize the horror of what was happening, I looked up again at the television and watched, incredulously, as a second plane flew into the second tower.

I ran back to my desk and called Joe who was at his office across the river. He didn't know what was happening. He could barely understand me. I told him to turn on the television, and then I hung up. Within minutes, he was watching the same news reports. I locked up my papers, ran down the Embassy's back set of stairs, and hurried outside to a tram that would eventually get me to my neighborhood.

The Embassy emptied out quickly. Everyone wanted to check on their families. Joe left his office. We both knew we had to get the kids. We arrived at their school at the same time. It was complete pandemonium, with parents and children running everywhere. School principals and teachers were trying to keep some kind of control in the halls. We found the children and walked across the street to our house. Once settled there, and before we sat the kids down to explain what was going on, or at least what we thought was happening, we tried to reach our families in the States. All the lines were blocked; the circuits were overloaded. It took hours to get through. Thankfully, before we went to bed for the night, we were able to reassure everyone we were okay and get confirmation they were safe. I was still very concerned for my older brother, though. He was an NYPD police officer, and I knew he was probably in the thick of the disaster. It took many hours before I learned that he, too, was safe but had been working around the clock at the site of the crashes.

We did our best to explain to the children what was happening. They didn't understand. Their comfortable world was suddenly turned upside down.

For years, the quest for any information regarding what exactly happened on the 11th of September 2001 consumed all of us in the CIA. Why had it happened, who was responsible and how would the US respond? We were tasked to find anyone with even a nugget of information that might help piece together what had occurred and give us warning of any other potential threats against the US.

We held meeting after meeting with our assets. There was a real sense of urgency now. We analyzed data to make sure we had people who had good access to accurate information. People seemed to come out of the woodwork with "news" we had to vet, stories of things they thought they knew. Everything we were told had to be checked. It was overwhelming.

My workweek suddenly increased from sixty hours a week to eighty. No one slept. There was no time for sleep. I was running on caffeine and adrenaline, sometimes on autopilot. I wondered when I'd get a break or if things would ever ease up. I'd get a call, a message, or a note saying there was another agent to meet, another lead to follow. It was never-ending, and something had to give.

At least at home, all was well with the children…for now.

Chapter Seventeen

The Wanderer

Around the World
2000-2008

Losing important items like our video camera or even whole pieces of luggage, although bothersome and worrisome at times, was typical of our hectic and somewhat nomadic lifestyle. With so many moving parts, so many changes, so many boxes being packed and new houses to set up, so many new people to meet and neighborhoods to navigate, so many cities and towns to explore, and so many activities to keep track of, we were bound to lose things now and then.

Losing children, though? That was a whole different story. Eric, our very free-spirited son, seemed to have an inclination for wandering off. When he was still a small baby snuggled safely in our child carrier backpack, all was well.

We explored Malta as a family of five. We walked through Valletta, Malta's capital, down to the island's rocky beaches, watched the bobbing wooden fishing boats in bright reds, yellows, and blues and, on the bows of each, a tiny pair of painted eyes. We hopped on the famous yellow buses that allowed us to move faster around the island. Everywhere we looked was the beautiful blue color of the Mediterranean. We soaked in Malta's long history as we explored churches, fortresses, and the narrow streets of the towns. It was sometimes hard to decipher the banter we heard all around us. The English that the Maltese spoke was interspersed with Arabic and Italian.

It was easy to keep track of three small children, holding tight to their hands and watching Eric enjoy the view from the backpack Joe carried him in.

But…as Eric grew, so did his tendency to wander.

He was never so much lost as out of touch for a bit. I would argue this was neither a sign of bad parenting nor of having too many children. It was, in the end, just an idiosyncrasy of our nomadic and unusual life…and maybe a little bit due to Eric's proclivity to roam.

Leaving him behind in the Pizza Hut in Egypt was just the first of many such incidents.

Through the years between my assignments overseas, we'd often join family for beach vacations on the Delaware shore. The cousins loved this time together, where they'd run from the beach to the pool to the lake then start all over again. During those years, my father relished seeing all his children and grandchildren together. To him, family was the most important.

The beach in Delaware was wide and beautiful, and the ocean was powerful and gray. The weeks we spent there were carefree and fun. The children played hard, then collapsed at night to ready themselves for another full day of unrestrained fun. Dinners together had the adults in one room contemplating the next day's agenda, with "important" items to be considered, such as should we start our day at the pool or the beach, while the kids regaled each other with jokes that only they understood.

The cousins ran between our rented houses, fished at the lakes on the property, rode on the trolley around the resort, and played on the tennis and basketball courts a few cul-de-sacs away. They all watched out for each other, more or less.

One sunny afternoon, as we enjoyed our little corner of the beach, we noticed Eric was missing…again! We were sure he was close by, somewhere between us and the water. Then, as the seconds and then minutes passed and the crowds became too thick to see more than a few beach umbrellas away, we ran to the lifeguards.

We gathered up all our family members and began walking the very busy shoreline, all the while keeping one scared eye on the powerful waves crashing on the beach. Could he have been swept under the current? Could he have been scooped up by some nefarious person?

Finally, after a very long twenty minutes, we saw a kind, middle-aged woman carrying flip-flops in one hand and holding a little boy with the other. They were heading towards us and navigating a sea of sunbathers oblivious to the crisis that was just averted. Eric was calm. When we grabbed him and hugged him, he didn't seem to understand why we were so upset. We're still not sure how Eric or the lovely woman found us among all those people. It was nothing short of a miracle that we were so quickly reunited.

Until it happened again.

The children were great little skiers by the early 2000s. We planned to spend a fun-filled weekend day at Jiminy Peak Mountain in the Berkshires. We were ready to tackle the thin cover of snow over layers of ice that was so typical of East Coast skiing. It wasn't the Alps, but it *was* a glorious sunny day, and the mountain was ready for us.

Skiing midday, when temperatures are starting to rise and there is a clear view across the peaks, always creates a lively, gleeful, almost festive atmosphere. The glistening snow, the bright sun, the ruddy faces, the loud rock and roll blasting from the lodge...you can't help but be invigorated and in a good mood.

Katrina and Alexis were in daycare and ski school, respectively. Joe and I were skiing with the three older children. We all went up and came down again and again. After one particularly exhilarating run, Joe reached the bottom before the rest of us. He waited near the lift, anxious to gather the group and head back up for another pass. I came down next, and then, together, we looked up to beckon the others in our direction. Claire arrived, then Kyle. Then we waited...and waited. Minutes passed, and we lost our place in line. We collectively rolled our eyes and, with more than a bit of frustration, began to murmur, "Here we go again."

The time continued to pass. Still no Eric. We knew he hadn't beaten us to the bottom. He hadn't skied past us. We scanned the hill. There was only one way down. So where was he? We sent Claire and Kyle back up the chairlift so they could make another sweep down while we waited at the bottom. All bases were covered. We would certainly intercept him one way or the other. As more minutes ticked by, though, we became seriously concerned. We flagged a ski patrol and, trying to keep our panic at a controlled level, told them our son didn't make it down the hill. Then we waited some more, becoming increasingly worried as the afternoon sun waned. Claire and Kyle had reached the bottom again without spotting Eric and now started to complain they were missing out on runs.

Then, out of nowhere it seemed, Eric appeared in front of us! He was perfectly fine. He had been found by the ski patrol walking *up* the hill after having lost his skis on a tumble. They had loaded him onto a toboggan and pulled him down the mountain. He showed up at the bottom, euphoric and, frankly, proud of himself for having survived his adventure. We were filled with relief. All his brother, Kyle, could mutter was, "How come *he* got a toboggan ride down?"

LEGOLAND, near Munich, Germany, was supposed to be just another fun-filled day. The creative, interactive, outdoor expanse of a park, with a bit of a Disney feel to it, was packed with children holding onto their parents with one hand and carrying their favorite Lego toy in the other.

Life-sized Lego characters walked among the Lego sculptures. Stores beckoned parents to spend another few Deutschmarks to make their children happy. Fast-food stands sold fun-looking but very unhealthy snacks. There was so much activity, so many distractions, but all in the spirit of having a perfectly enjoyable day with the family. What could possibly go wrong?

Meandering down the main street of the park, soaking up the ambiance and watching all the activity around us, we were thinking of stopping for an ice cream when, suddenly, we were missing a child. A few minutes earlier, Eric had slowed down to watch a play being performed by several dressed-up characters, so Joe and I had moved to a nearby table to sit for a minute and wait. When the play was over, we stood up to continue to the next ride. We had Claire and Kyle but…not Eric. Where was he?

This time, Eric was missing a bit longer than normal, and real worry began to set in. We told Claire to stay with Kyle and Alexis (Katrina had not been born yet). Joe and I began the search, starting out in different directions and coming back to the children every few minutes to make sure we didn't lose anyone else. Finally, Joe, somewhat hesitatingly, took the necessary next step and reported Eric missing to park security.

Not long after asking for help, thankfully, I found Eric sitting on a bench between two pleasant-faced LEGOLAND employees. This time, though, he wasn't smiling, and he wasn't proud of himself. Rather, he was sobbing uncontrollably. The employees were trying hard to comfort him, asking his name, showing him little Lego pieces and trying to convince him not to worry. But Eric wasn't having any of it. He was crying so hard he couldn't even catch his breath enough to be able to answer their questions.

Following this last little disaster, we did what all good parents would do and held regular practice question-and-answer sessions with our children. We regularly ran down the list of critical information—name, phone numbers, emergency contacts—and had the kids repeat it over and over. We really didn't want the disappearance act to happen again.

Yet…it did. There continued to be more of these kinds of Eric episodes. The next one, unfortunately, happened at Frankfurt Airport, one of the world's busiest hubs. Four different concourses joined at the Terminal One intersection where passengers arriving from and leaving on hundreds of international and domestic flights moved through at lightning speed as if trying to catch the last plane available.

Every traveler seemed to be looking straight ahead. So much activity. Everyone was moving so fast. How did they all know where they needed to go? It was as if each person was caught up in the same wave of humanity and carried along, crisscrossing the intersection, stepping over and around obstacles without even thinking. Then Eric, too, got swept away in the sea of bodies and fast-moving feet.

It was inevitable that with five children, fourteen suitcases, seven carry-ons, plus Adrienne and her large dog crate, something was bound to get lost.

We were hunkered together in a tiny spot near two pillars just a few yards from the Lufthansa check-in counter. We all waited there for Joe to come back with boarding passes and luggage tags. As he turned toward us, though, something caught his eye over the tops of our heads. Eric was walking away from our group, oblivious to all the activity around him.

Joe dropped the boarding passes, the passports, and the luggage tags back onto the counter and ran through the crowd, keeping his eyes focused on Eric. I watched through the throng of people. I saw him reach down, scoop Eric up, then make his way back to us. He calmly set Eric down next to Adrienne and the rest of us and exhaled with relief. Eric, still unaware of the tenuous situation he had just avoided, simply carried on with his babbling.

Every time, these moments began with a bit of irritation—the "here we go again" kind of annoyance. Then, as the minutes wore on, our agitation turned to genuine frustration—the kind all parents routinely deal with when it comes to their children. Then, the temporary frustration would quickly evolve into real worry and, ultimately, panic.

In the end, Eric was always found, and we often joke now about his penchant for getting lost around the world.

Eric kept us on our toes and put our parental skills to the test.

Chapter Eighteen

Health Crisis

Europe
2000-2011

In August 2000 we were getting ready to move on from North Africa to our assignment in Central Europe. Another few years ahead of us, full of opportunities. There were lots of potential targets in and near this city for me to try to meet and recruit. I had learned a bit of the local language, at least enough to ask for directions and buy milk. We knew what house we were moving into. The kids were set to begin the school year in yet another new place.

With every move, most of our household goods and assorted furniture went into storage. The rest of our possessions were on a ship somewhere in the middle of the Atlantic. And as usual, we were living out of suitcases in a long-term hotel. It was a regular requirement that ahead of every move overseas, my family had to be medically cleared for travel. We had been through this process many times—just another hurdle before we could board the plane.

This time, though, it wasn't going to be quick and simple. Something was wrong.

Joe went in for his exam. I stayed in the waiting room with the three kids. My pregnancy with number four was making me naturally anxious and uncomfortable. I expected Joe to be finished within ten or fifteen minutes. We still had a lot to do—purchases to make, documents to check, people to see. The schedule seemed endless.

But instead, I was called back to the exam room where Joe was with the doctor. I became a little irritated. What was the delay now? I asked the receptionist to keep an eye on the children in the waiting room and strode down the narrow hall. Joe was sitting on the exam table facing the doctor. This was unusual, I thought to myself. I was still a bit annoyed as we really didn't have time to waste.

I watched as the gray-haired doctor with a worn face probed at Joe's throat and around the sides of his neck again and again. The doctor didn't seem to like what he saw—I could tell by the frown slowly forming on his face.

He said Joe needed additional tests. There was an anomaly on his neck. The doctor then added, as if wanting to counter the pushback forming on my lips, that it was significant enough to have it checked more thoroughly.

Joe fired back quickly, thanking the doctor but explaining that we already had airplane tickets to travel and would be leaving in a couple of days. I weighed in and said that of course I would make sure Joe went to a specialist as soon as we arrived at our destination.

This elderly doctor that I wanted to immediately dismiss looked directly at the two of us and slowly shook his head. As he walked over to the sink in the exam room to wash his hands, he turned to Joe and said as firmly as he could, "You're not going anywhere, at least not until you get this looked at."

Joe argued, "But you don't understand. My wife's job overseas starts this week. We need to go…" His words trailed off as the doctor's head continued to shake back and forth.

"There's a lump on your thyroid," the doctor said soberly, crossing his arms as if to punctuate his thoughts. "You need more tests to see if it's cancer before you're able to travel. It's not negotiable. You don't get to decide when you go."

"Wha…what?" Joe was aghast.

I sat down abruptly to catch my breath. *Well, this is unexpected.* Then I thought, *This could be bad, really bad.*

The next few days were a blur. We scrambled, called doctors, called our families. We felt alone. We didn't know what to do first. We didn't have a plan. None of the organizing I had done over the past months was helpful now. I called the medical unit in my office repeatedly, asking for assistance.

"You need an endocrinologist for your husband," they said matter-of-factly.

"Is there a list?" I pleaded.

I called one endocrinologist who was a regular in their office, but when I requested an appointment, I was told, "We can see your husband in September."

It was July. Not only were we discussing a life-threatening disease, but somehow, we also had to continue with our plans of relocating abroad. *How could they not have any appointments for three months?!* This was unacceptable. I had someplace to be. I had my next assignment to start. The children had to begin school.

Things seemed to be falling apart.

The doctor tried to make us feel better by telling us, "If you're going to have a cancerous lump, the thyroid is where you want it to be." He was wrong. That definitely did NOT make us feel any better.

Our family in New York knew some doctors at our hometown hospital and, thankfully, were able to get Joe an appointment within the week. At least he was in the system for the next step. Following the scheduling of that first appointment, time seemed to pass so slowly. Every few days, we checked in with my office to explain the delay. Eventually, Joe underwent a thin needle biopsy.

It was inconclusive, so the surgeons decided to probe further. There were more tests to schedule. More time passed.

What we feared came true—Joe would have to have the lump removed. It was malignant. Now, things moved with urgency. He was prepped for surgery. We learned afterward that the surgeon decided while Joe was under anesthesia, in an abundance of caution, to take out his entire thyroid.

Following the successful surgery, we all moved in with my in-laws in New York while Joe recuperated and, together, we spent the next several weeks working through this very unexpected wrinkle in our plans.

Despite the delays and the hassle, we knew that this bothersome health requirement clearly saved Joe's life.

Three years later, we were again back in America between assignments. Life, now with five children, was moving along. We had our routine—work, school, life.

Once again in an instant, everything changed.

It began with an excruciating pain in my left eye. I went to the emergency room, then to my eye doctor, then to an ophthalmologist. Each doctor seemed increasingly concerned.

Then, the diagnosis came—multiple sclerosis.

Over those first few weeks, I learned that the severe bout of optic neuritis I had was linked to a brief period of paralysis in my legs that I had experienced a few weeks prior. I underwent all kinds of neurological tests, including an MRI, that ultimately confirmed the diagnosis.

What did this mean? How did this happen? How would I continue working? Was this a death sentence?

I still had a long career ahead of me, or so I thought. I had five children between the ages of one and eleven to raise, and a husband I wanted to spend more time with.

I found myself researching doctors, scheduling appointments with specialists in different states, and talking to college friends who were in the medical field. I was desperate to find out why this happened and how serious it could be. I wanted to know if perhaps there had been a mistake, that maybe everything had been blown way out of proportion.

Instead, I kept getting sent for more tests—a constant flurry of MRIs, CT scans, blood tests, and sensory and balance assessments, all checking for neurological discrepancies. There were serious talks with Joe. He was as confused as I was. How would we plan for our future now? We were stunned.

It wasn't until years later that I even broached the topic with the children. *They don't need to worry*, I said to myself. There was nothing they could do to change things. They didn't need to think about their mother being sick. What difference would it make? This was something I grappled with over the years. Why add to their struggles and concerns? Anyway…mothers weren't supposed to get sick, right?

Since that fateful day in late 2003, I rarely talk about how the disease has affected my life. I have struggled physically but not in the debilitating ways that many afflicted with MS suffer. I am still very much able to walk and talk and think. I always wanted to run another marathon. I wanted to be sure the first one I ran wasn't a fluke. I wanted to know I could do it again. But running is difficult for me now. The increased heat in my muscles that occurs with serious exercise exacerbates the MS symptoms.

Over the years, I have regularly suffered from migraines as well as extreme fatigue. I have found a way to manage the headaches when the nausea or out-of-sorts feeling begins. I have also found a way to manage the fatigue. I consider these hassles minor compared to what I could be experiencing with this disease.

Sometimes, when I am driving and suddenly get overwhelmingly tired, I'll pull off the road into a parking lot and take a ten-minute nap. At work, I'd be lucky enough to be able to keep going through the day or evening or night, but then I'd often hit a wall.

For almost eight years after the diagnosis, I gave myself intramuscular injections in an effort to keep the effects of the MS under control. The injections were weekly at first, then when I had to change medication, they were three times a week. Sometimes, I'd give myself shots in my thighs, sometimes in my stomach or my hips. Other places on my body were too hard to reach or too unbearably painful. The injections left big, ugly, blue welts all over me.

I hated this part. I had difficulty placing the auto-injector close enough to my skin to get the medicine into the muscle. I hesitated. I squirmed. I wavered. I gave up and walked away; then, I'd try again until I could finally bring myself to push the button. While the pain of the needle and the medicine entering my body was very real, the mental frustration was often more difficult to overcome than anything else. This wasn't temporary. I had to learn to live with it. I also knew—or wanted to believe—that the discomfort, pain, and inconvenience I was experiencing just might help me to remain mobile long enough until my children could take care of themselves.

I looked strange with large, swollen bruises all over my body, but I had to stay on a schedule. I meticulously planned meetings around my injection days. I wanted to be alone, somewhere private, and calm for those few minutes that I needed to give myself a shot. Some days were more difficult than others. As usual I found myself juggling meetings and activities, but now it was not just to make one of my children's school performances; this was to keep myself moving, to keep myself upright and walking.

I was determined to continue working as hard and as long as everyone else. When I had a migraine, I took a pill and hoped it would pass. When I was tired and couldn't seem to function one more minute, I pushed through until I had an opportunity to lie down at home. When I had to take injections three times a week and was in the office, I asked the medics in the Embassy clinic to help me.

The nurses always had my injection ready. They knew I was busy and didn't have time to waste. They didn't hesitate or hover the needle over my skin. They were professional. They never let me put it off.

I had to plan ahead when I traveled. I couldn't skip any injections, so I carried the medicine in a cooler with an ice pack along with documentation to explain why I was boarding an airplane with hypodermic needles.

Almost seven years after I was first diagnosed, and while still living overseas, I learned that an oral drug for MS was in the process of being approved by the US Food and Drug Administration (FDA). The drug was already available in Europe to those who knew about it. I was having progressively more difficulty handling the pain that the injections inflicted. I was eager to stop being poked by needles. Even after so many years of administering the medicine, I continued to have a mental block about putting the needle into my body.

"I can't continue like this," I complained over and over to my neurologist. He was an expert in MS. I liked and respected him. His office was crowded with journal articles, scientific magazines, and charts. Once past the disarray, though, and sitting across from him at his desk, I felt a calm envelop me. He had a confident, caring air about him that always put me at ease.

He was never in a hurry. I told him what I was feeling. I grumbled about my complicated lifestyle with the medicine and the distress it caused me. He knew I was reaching a breaking point.

"My life already has so much going on, and now I'm constantly consumed with worry about whether all the pain I'm going through with the shots is even helping. There's got to be a better way."

That's when he told me about the new medicine. "There is an oral drug on the market," he said hesitantly, "but there are risks. It's so new, not much is yet known about its side effects or even how well it works."

Without any hesitation, I asked, "What can I do to get it?"

The idea of no more injections was so appealing I was ready to do whatever it took to make it work. I begged. "I need to try it."

"The drug is showing evidence of slowing the heart rate," he emphasized, adding, "You need to be aware that it has not been fully tested yet."

"I still want to try it," I continued anxiously.

My neurologist expressed concern, but ultimately agreed. "Okay, let's move ahead."

Relief washed over me. I knew I had to continue taking the medicine, but the injections were becoming impossible to sustain. Finally, I felt there was some hope for me.

I was strictly observed by my doctor as I received the first dose, then tested regularly to monitor my white blood cell count and vitamin D levels.

This new drug completely changed my life for the better. The FDA eventually approved it for distribution in the US. Fortunately, I was already ahead of the game.

Those years were a dark time for me. I felt alone, facing this disease and its unknown effects by myself. I didn't really know how bad it would get, and I wondered every day if my children might somehow be genetically predisposed to MS.

As usual, though, I didn't have too much time to think, worry, or feel sorry for myself. It was again time to move to another country.

Chapter Nineteen

Armed and Dangerous

Europe
2008-2011

By the summer of 2008, there were seven of us. The children were now growing into little people, each with their own personalities. We were huddled together for many weeks in two small rooms in a Northern Virginia hotel, waiting for the final approvals to be signed so we could get on another plane and head to our next destination.

This assignment was going to be different, though. I was going to be the second in command of a large office. My boss was solid. I liked and respected him. I knew we would do great things. Work was going to be terrific—very busy, but terrific.

The Southern European country we were headed to was dealing with a formidable mass migration problem. Streams of people poured onto their shores from Iraq and Afghanistan, then made their way north further into Europe. Most of them were just hoping to start a new life. The situation, though, was turning into an economic and humanitarian catastrophe. Housing, food, and medical care were insufficient to accommodate the huge influx of people. Borders were being overrun.

Police and federal authorities were losing control. Law enforcement needed help keeping track of who was coming in and who was leaving. The large number of people crossing into the country, even though most were simply seeking a better life, created a significant risk that someone, even just one person with bad intentions, could be hiding in the crowds.

We were trying to help our foreign partners process the massive numbers, if for no other reason than to ensure someone who wanted to cause damage—or even kill—didn't get through the system undetected. Our databases were tied to a vast, worldwide network of details about people and organizations considered to be dangerous. Thankfully, we were sometimes able to track individuals and find connections between them that provided enough information to disrupt the plan of an attack.

For the next three years, because of a number of perceived threats surrounding the country we were in, as well as from within its own borders, I drove an armored SUV and carried a 9mm Glock. My vehicle was heavy, solid, and sometimes difficult to maneuver. When the children climbed into the back seat, they struggled to close the door. To them, it was clearly seen as more of a nuisance than protection for their mom. Their friends never understood why our car seemed so different from every other car they had been in before.

I had very few outfits that came with a belt, and even if they did, the belt would not have held a holster. Since I was required to have my Glock with me whenever I was working outside the office, two of our technical officers did me a huge favor. They reconfigured my go-to, large, black Coach purse so that I could easily access my weapon whenever it was necessary. It also allowed me to inconspicuously carry it with me wherever I went. When the tech officers had completed their complicated sewing job, I was able to conceal my weapon and still use my bag every day to carry my notebook, wallet, keys, and lunch.

Essentially, these talented officers created a hidden compartment that securely held my gun. It worked beautifully. I practiced holding my bag in different positions and reaching for, pulling out, then aiming the weapon. To keep my shooting skills fresh, I joined colleagues once a month at a range outside of the city to practice target shooting against a huge dirt embankment.

As part of our weekly schedule, my boss and I met regularly with the local FBI Legal Attaché, Andy. He had been in this European country a year or two before I arrived. He understood what the CIA was trying to do there and appreciated the different roles between us and his organization. He was smart and had been an FBI agent for almost two decades. He was also a good family man.

We provided Andy with information from our sources that helped him track down leads of interest to the FBI while he gave us pertinent details obtained from his many Interpol contacts. Together, we honed in on suspected terrorist groups or nefarious individuals. Once we had solid information that could be used in a prosecution, our local liaison partners made the arrest. Our combined efforts thwarted many dangerous situations—although exact details of what we did and how we did it never became known outside our circles. None of us could risk losing the sources that provided the information leading to a disruption of a terrorist threat.

In our line of work, things didn't always happen during the day. Luckily, Andy lived only about ten minutes from me. I periodically had to stop by his house and interrupt his family dinnertime to give him a five-minute update on something happening. Situations changed rapidly. I often couldn't wait until the next morning to pass along the information.

My boss and I also met weekly with the Ambassador and the DCM. We briefed them on some of our clandestine operations, specifically, those that would have extremely negative repercussions on them or the country we were in if they became known outside our office.

We were lucky. Both the Ambassador and the DCM were on our side. We didn't tell them everything we were doing, but they trusted us. They understood that if there was something they needed to know, we would find them and, without hesitation, brief them.

One weekend, we learned that an individual we had been monitoring for several months had just crossed into the country. We had been keeping the Ambassador informed about the person's travels in the region. Now, not only was he close, but we also had concerns about his reasons for being in the country.

My boss was out of town. I called the direct number of the Ambassador's residence. I gave the switchboard operator my name and office, told him I needed to speak to the Ambassador immediately, and asked if I could come to the residence within the next thirty minutes. The Ambassador lived in a stately building surrounded by lush gardens with a circular drive leading to the front entrance. It had been home to the US ambassadors in that country for years.

The residence was only a block from the Embassy. I parked in the garage on the Embassy compound and walked up the hill. It was late, about 11 p.m. on a Friday. The Ambassador himself answered the door then ushered me into the sitting room. We spoke for only a few minutes. I gave him an update on the individual we had been tracking, including our work that day with the police. They knew where he was bedded down. They planned to make the arrest that night.

I spent several minutes recounting for the Ambassador what we knew about the individual. I explained again, this time in more detail, that he was a senior decision-maker with the group Al-Qaeda in the Arabian Peninsula (AQAP), designated a terrorist organization by the US in January 2010, less than six months earlier. The group, a Sunni extremist sect based in Yemen, had already orchestrated several high-profile terrorist attacks against Western interests in the Arabian Peninsula and further abroad. We didn't have any details as to why this AQAP member was in Europe, but we had developed a convincing enough package for the local police to make the arrest.

I left the Ambassador's residence and walked back to my office at the Embassy to check for the latest updates. It was going to be a long night. I stayed close to my phone throughout the early morning hours as our police contacts provided me with details of their surveillance of the individual and the ultimate arrest. The operation was a perfect example of the joint working relationship we had spent a lot of time developing with local law enforcement.

Despite the good work with our liaison partners, we were still on edge. Not only were we trying to keep track of terrorist groups around the world, but there were issues closer to home to contend with as well. An indigenous organization had perpetrated attacks against the foreign and local population in this country over the past twenty years. We were always concerned, wondering if or when another attack would happen, and, if so, where.

Every November, a large, volatile group held marches throughout the city. The reason for these yearly protests began more than thirty years before, in November 1973, with a massive student demonstration rejecting a military-style rule. Following a tank crashing through the gates of the university, bloodshed ensued, and many students were killed. The annual march, held every November 17th, commemorates that 1973 uprising. And every year, our office was on high alert leading up to the event and for the entire day and night of the protests.

As a precautionary measure, all businesses and schools closed; Embassy personnel were prohibited from going into the city center that day; and everyone was directed to hunker down in their homes.

Nonetheless, despite all the threats that seemed to be around every corner, family activities continued.

There was the day I met our new puppy, Roy (aka Royale with Cheese). Returning from another weeklong business trip back to the US, I parked in our garage, grabbed my bag out of the trunk, walked up the sidewalk along the driveway, climbed the steps, and entered through the front door. As I walked in, Joe and four of our kids were standing together in a row just inside the hall. They had slight smirks on their faces…then…I heard it. A soft, distant snorting sound coming from the small bathroom located under the stairs, just behind the children. Suddenly, not being able to contain themselves any longer, the kids started to giggle. They ran to the bathroom and pulled open the door.

Out scurried a tiny, black puppy. He was so small he could have been mistaken for a little rat. He blended in perfectly with the black-and-white tiled floor of the foyer. At first, I wasn't sure what was happening. Then Eric picked him up and began to cuddle him in his arms. Soon, I learned Roy's background. Joe had negotiated with one of the nurses in the Embassy clinic who was a breeder of miniature pinschers, and, for one hundred euros, picked out Roy from the litter.

Apparently, as Joe and the children drove back to the house with their new puppy comfortably ensconced in one of their laps, they had discussed names. It was supposedly the children's decision, but Joe made the first suggestion, stating that since he was so small maybe he should be known as "Big Mac." At that very moment, they were passing by a McDonald's restaurant. Since Joe is a big fan of the fast-food chain, he thought it made sense. Thankfully, though, the kids already knew a dog named Mac, so they vetoed that option. Then Joe suggested "Royale with Cheese," a reference from one of his favorite films, *Pulp Fiction*. There it was—Royale with Cheese, or just "Roy" to his friends and family. I wasn't consulted, and it was too late because Roy seemed to already answer to his new name.

Music from our Bösendorfer grand piano poured throughout the house in those days. It raised everyone's mood. The children played after school, and as the house filled with party guests, the piano created an ambience that made everyone come together and sing.

Our Christmas traditions followed us wherever we went. We usually managed to find at least some of our favorite holiday foods. We pulled out decorations from boxes we had mailed to ourselves and dug deep into the closets to find the children's stockings to hang on the staircase.

In the winter of 2010, we entertained hundreds of guests at our home for a Christmas season gala. The invite list for this big work event included friends, my colleagues, Joe's colleagues, local officials, neighbors, parents of our children's friends, acquaintances, other expatriates we knew, and even friends from the US who were visiting us for a few weeks.

Outside, our house was adorned with dozens of white and red poinsettias that lined the steps to our front door, ornamenting the terrace and all the pathways. Trees dotted with lights flickered and glistened throughout the garden. The driveway leading to the house, as well as the yard, terrace, garage, and walkways had all been swept by bomb-sniffing dogs to ensure there wouldn't be any unexpected incidents. Our security team was stationed outside the gated front entrance to watch for anomalies. The US Ambassador stopped by with his own security team. Welcome drinks were passed to the guests. There was excitement in the air.

The inside of the house was decorated with hundreds of lights, green garland, and more poinsettias bordering both sides of the front staircase. The caterers were busy prepping hors d'oeuvres. The servers were already hustling along a path they had created from the garage area, where they had set up their trays, through the basement rooms and up the stairs to the kitchen. Everything moved like clockwork.

Claire was in the middle of high school when we arrived here, a tough period for any adolescent anywhere. This time though, for Claire, it was worse than just being a teenager in high school. We had dragged Claire across the ocean to an entirely new school in a new country where they spoke a different language. She was so sad those first few days in our new home. She missed her routine. She missed her friends. Even though just outside her bedroom window there was a massive palm tree, and even though the sky was always blue, the sun was always shining, and the beach was only fifteen minutes away, she still cried inconsolably for the life she had just left.

To see her so sad at the beginning of this assignment broke my heart. If she was unhappy, what did that mean for everyone else? Was I the only one excited to be here? Was I the only one looking forward to what lay ahead?

This was the same Claire, though, who a few years later went to university in France, found professional work in Greece, then relocated there permanently. We didn't realize, of course, during those nights listening to her sob that all would be well if we were just a little bit patient. We again questioned whether "dragging" the kids around the world was really the right thing to do.

Claire continued to dance throughout these years. She first started ballet when she was only five and back in the US. She was good at it and enjoyed the performances. All the girls got to wear colorful, shimmering costumes that dazzled the proud parents sitting in the audience.

Within the first few weeks of arriving in this Southern European country, we found a dance studio only a short drive from our house. The school was located on the ground floor of a narrow, nondescript apartment building off a very busy main road. The instructor spoke some French, but the students and all their parents only spoke the local language. The tiny studio was full of energy and life. Walking through the front door, children scurried everywhere as they prepared for class or changed out of their pointe shoes and readied to head home. The parents seemed to know one another already. Not long after Claire began dancing at this studio, her class performed on a big stage at the renowned music hall in the center of the city.

Claire moved from place to place more than any of the other children simply by virtue of the fact she was our firstborn. She, like the others, always left behind good friends, a comfortable life, and routines to which she had become accustomed. Also, like the others, she always eventually developed a whole new group of friends. Claire had a healthy social life. She was comfortable meeting new people. She became adept at getting around any city by public transportation or taxi. We relied on Claire. She was the big sister to four siblings. She was responsible for ensuring they were okay when we weren't nearby, and she was always up to the task.

Still in elementary school, Alexis and her entrepreneurial interests were taking off. She started A's Work-It Shop, creating art pieces for sale. She had quite the family following. One day, however, the "business control officials" came by in suit jackets (and shorts) and with no explanation or justified reasoning, shut Alexis' new business down. Eric and Kyle, both carrying clipboards, produced some questionable documentation that confirmed A's Work-It Shop had to close. When pressed for an explanation, they cited a vague—and clearly fabricated—violation. I tried to intervene and asked for their proof. They continued, playfully stating there was no going back. Finally, I pulled Alexis aside and assured her I'd still purchase her creations no matter what.

The boys eventually had other, more important matters to attend to. That first year, they both got braces. Dr. George, the orthodontist, was a boisterous, gregarious, and friendly man. He had dual citizenship and had only been back in the country for about ten years. His wife, Patty, was always volunteering at the school. Visits to Dr. George were easy, and paying was on a typically flexible, honor code kind of schedule. As couples, we socialized together, the kids played together, we attended the same official functions and school events, and we always seemed to cross paths at the supermarket.

With so many children in the house, we always ran out of one grocery item or another before the weekend. For the quick, emergency purchase, there were small kiosks on every street corner throughout every neighborhood. They offered a little bit of everything and always seemed to be open. The nearest one to us was two blocks in the direction of the main road. Just about every week we sent one of the children to the corner stand with two euros to bring home a bottle of milk, incentivizing them with a few extra coins to buy an ice cream for themselves.

We could see that they were happy and having fun, but were we asking too much of them? Were we expecting too much?

CHAPTER TWENTY

FAMILY DYNAMICS

Around the World
1994-2011

When we were first married, Joe and I never discussed any specific plan for our life together. We weren't exactly sure what the next ten, twenty, thirty, or forty years would look like. Would we have children? If so, how many? Would we travel? Would we stay in one house? What kind of life would we have if we didn't have children? Whose career would take priority and for how long? What would our careers look like? Where would we live? Where would we vacation?

Along the way, we never questioned what we were doing or why. Instead, we moved and then moved again. We had children, one after another. Throughout our journey, we had lots of hopes, dreams, and ideas for each of them. We wanted to see the children grow up to take advantage of every moment. We wanted them to get jobs and have experiences that would be purposeful—that would mean something, be worth something. We wanted them to engage in opportunities and jump into adventures that they would remember forever.

There were times we needed help, though. I knew that whether we were back in Paris someday or in another European city or somewhere in Africa or even in another corner of the US, we would find good neighbors and make lifelong friends and be able to turn to them when we needed to. Whatever their nationality, whatever language they spoke, these neighbors became our support system. We needed them. Our children knew that, and they knew who to go to when we weren't there.

One weekday, early on in one of our overseas assignments, Joe and I were both at work. Joe was in his office at the American school, and I was on the road, preparing for a meeting. I was out of touch for the day. We had been in our new house in our new neighborhood for less than a week.

All five children arrived back home after their third day at a new school in this foreign country. As was the established plan, they were let off the bus on the side of the road directly in front of our house. A thick, solid stone wall surrounded our property with a black metal gate that extended across the driveway. The small pedestrian door that was part of the bigger black gate opened into the front garden. This door was locked from the outside, but there was a bell to the left of the handle. Outside the gate, at the top of the wall facing down, was a camera that alerted us from inside the house who was there.

As soon as the children spilled off the bus, Claire realized she didn't have a key. In fact, we hadn't made any extra keys yet but thought that if we weren't home, at least our nanny would be there to let the children in after school. The keys were the heavy, antique brass ones that were difficult to replicate, so it took time to find someone who could do the job.

The children rang the doorbell, but no one answered. No one was home. Joe and I were both situated in our respective offices, trying to learn our new jobs, and our nanny hadn't arrived at the house yet. We lived on a quiet street, so five small children, none of whom spoke the language, milling around in front of the property, probably looked a bit out of the ordinary.

Kyle, our confident middle schooler, took charge. He climbed over the wall and jumped down into the front yard below. He continued up ten wide steps leading to the front door and knocked. Again, no one answered.

"Kyle, go around to the back!" the others yelled. He followed the path to the right, through the side garden to the back terrace and tried the kitchen door. It, too, was locked. Kyle returned to the front and climbed back over the fence to rejoin his siblings, lamenting that they all just had to wait.

Claire took over. "Let's try the house across the street. Maybe they speak English and can help." They all dashed across and knocked on the neighbor's house. None of the children were really that concerned. No one had a plan of what to do next if the neighbors weren't home, didn't speak English, or didn't want to talk to a bunch of kids. The problem was not insurmountable. It was just something to be dealt with.

Gabriella and George had lived in the house facing ours for years, but we hadn't met them yet. We found out later that they were quite well-known in the community. George had a prominent psychology practice in the city, and Gabriella was an artist and active in local politics. In fact, she was running for mayor of the neighborhood.

Without any hesitation, they welcomed our vagabond group into their home, and immediately provided them with a cool, refreshing drink, reassuring conversation, and, most importantly, a telephone.

Over the years, since that first encounter between George and Gabriella and our children, we have spent many long evenings with them talking about world politics, dancing at their famous house parties, dining in their well-appointed home decorated with exquisite pottery pieces that Gabriella handcrafted, and laughing over cocktails in their verdant backyard. The endearing bond we created with the "couple across the street" still lasts.

One day in March, these same friends gave our daughter, Alexis, the simplest of gifts for her birthday—a basket overflowing with plump, bright yellow lemons picked right off their backyard tree. It was a kind and elegant gesture. It was sophisticated, just like Gabriella and George, and it reflected the kind of people they were—uncomplicated, down-to-earth, stylish, and classy.

Throughout the years, our children became each other's playmates and best friends. They watched out for each other. Sometimes it seemed as if we were like the Von Trapp family from *The Sound of Music*, especially when they put on their own theater productions. One child was the director, barking orders about where people should sit or stand, while another handled the music for the "orchestra," ensuring the stereo had the right kind of music playing and at the right decibel level. One of the kids was a mom, another a dad, the others their children. Or one a queen, another a king, and the others their subjects. Four of them were performers in a spectacle, while the fifth was an emcee.

Their togetherness was particularly evident when we skied together as a family. The Alps were often the closest mountain range to us, and when we were farther afield, we often traveled back to Garmisch in Southern Germany because it was familiar and a great place to vacation. Skiing confidently down one of the majestic mountains of the Alps, all in a line, we were like ducklings following their leader.

As the kids grew up, we loaded our car with all the winter accoutrements—gloves, scarves, ski pants, and coats—and headed to Mariazell, Austria, or back to the Zugspitz in Germany, or to Upstate New York, or Mont Tremblant in Québec, Canada. We loved spending all day in the snow. While it could be an expensive outing, we managed to keep costs under control by handing down ski equipment to one kid after another and rewearing items until they didn't fit anyone anymore. We dug into our "winter clothes box" for goggles and hand warmers. We packed snacks. We drove to the mountains whenever we could, skied off-peak days, and kept going until the chairlifts stopped for the day so we could get "just one more run in" and feel like we were getting our money's worth.

Watching two, then three, then four, then five children playing together made us laugh, warmed our hearts, and made us remember how grateful we should be. The children always stayed close friends with each other as we moved from city to city. They created games together, roughhoused together, taught each other, made fun of each other, laughed together, looked out for each other, and loved each other.

We really counted on Claire. As the oldest, she was the responsible one. She had to keep track of the others. She bore much of the supervisory burden in those days. Having built-in babysitters is a huge advantage to a big family. Once Claire left for college, the responsibility turned to Kyle and then eventually to Eric. By the time the boys were both in college, Alexis and Katrina were old enough to take care of themselves until we got home from work.

Growing up in a foreign country with both parents working outside the home at important, demanding jobs created a sense of independence and confidence in our kids—traits that often go beyond the average middle or high schooler's comfort level. Our children developed those characteristics out of necessity. Still today, they all continue to demonstrate the unique ability to think on their feet, handle unexpected circumstances, and be resourceful when they need to be.

There wasn't a parental roadmap for ensuring that these traits were successfully instilled in our children. It seemed they simply grew with every experience they had and with every person they encountered. It all seemed a bit random—the places we lived, the people we met, the paths we took—but looking back over it all, maybe it wasn't so random after all. Perhaps this was all part of God's plan.

There was never a time when the children seemed bored or lost or lacked something to do. Claire helped keep the others on the right path. She was fun, sweet, spirited, sociable, kind, always empathetic and very smart. She loved to read, dance, and spend time with friends.

At our house in North Africa in our lovely outdoor courtyard, we had two large turtles that Claire had "adopted." We never knew how the turtles had arrived there or if they would someday leave by the same route, but they became a fixture. Claire named them Sleepy and Walker, for obvious reasons. It was quite a job ensuring they were fed and entertained. Even when Claire was bitten on the mouth by one of them as she was helping it to eat a piece of lettuce, she never gave up her turtle-sitting duties.

Though we had nothing to compare her to, we just knew Claire was crushing all the infant and toddler milestones. As a little girl, she had an ever so slightly coy smile. As an adult, Claire still has that beautiful smile. Claire is incredibly respectful of everyone around her. Growing up, she was comfortable and confident in the company of adults. She has always been independent and grounded. She loves being a part of our family. It is easy to spend time with her.

Claire grew up overseas. Her experiences traveling, her interest in the world, her love of exploring, and her cosmopolitan attitude all made her plan to settle in Europe and start her career there, an obvious one.

Kyle is our sensitive child. I could always see his worries, joys, excitement, and anxiousness on his face. He has never liked to talk about his feelings, keeping them all inside. He is athletic and smart, worked hard, and always wanted to do the right thing by everyone he encountered. Most of all he is a good friend and a really good person.

I'm not sure when I first saw it take root, but if someone was in need, Kyle was right there to make it better. Throughout our time abroad, Kyle made close, true friends. They knew they could count on him. This meant, though, that all the moves, one after another after another, were perhaps more difficult for him. He forged deep relationships with his friends, ties that weren't meant to last only a couple of years.

Eric is also athletic and smart. He asks profound questions that make you really have to think, questions I often could not answer. His brain was always working overtime, and he was curious and persevering. When he had an idea, he carried it out and made it happen. Like with his brother, I didn't often see his emotions. I wonder if that was a by-product of being "independent"—not showing any "weakness" or sorrow. Eric has always been great about spending time with the family and is an integral part of who we are as a group.

Alexis can make us all laugh just by her presence alone. The way she tells a story with dramatic mannerisms, peculiar references, and varied intonations always makes her commentary hysterically funny. She is creative, full of energy, and has loads of friends. Alexis loves to explore and never gives up an opportunity to do, see, or experience something new.

Katrina is wise beyond her years. She has always been more serious and mature than her peers. She is confident in herself, incredibly motivated and persistent. She has clear goals and works hard to attain them. She is athletic, and when she has a full day of workouts and practices, she looks to do even more. She is soulful and is fine spending time by herself, in fact, often preferring that to being with people who are concerned only with material things. She is very caring and kind.

Sports often took center stage as the children grew up. Playing on teams allowed the kids to make friends overseas, get regular exercise, and gave us a chance to meet all kinds of people, including other parents—some of whom were perfect for the work I was doing. Whether it was lacrosse, gymnastics, dance, T-ball, baseball, wrestling, football, softball, field hockey, or swimming, the children all found their favorite sport. When it came to music, the children all learned the requisite recorder and, of course, piano on our beautiful Bösendorfer.

Over time, we established our own routines and traditions. Joe and I jostled for the privilege of reading a story to the children at bedtime, primarily so we could lie down in a warm, relaxing spot, cuddled next to a sleepy child and maybe drift off ourselves. This plan often backfired, especially once the kids realized we had fallen asleep before we reached the end of the first page.

We surprised Claire with a loft for her bed one year, though we soon realized it was a bit too close to the ceiling. She was happy, nonetheless, and excited to have her own spot way up high, but once Joe or I got up there to read her a story, we couldn't easily get down!

I often wondered if my children's oft-repeated traits of athleticism, independence, confidence, and internalization of their emotions had anything to do with the life we led or if it was all just happenstance. While we were close as a family, was that enough? Did we give the children enough attention? Did we listen to them enough? Did we guide them in the right direction?

Through all our doubts and fears as parents, Joe and I held fast to our faith. Attending Mass every week was important to us. Raising the children as practicing Catholics was a priority. We found great parishes wherever we lived.

In one city, we went to a beautiful church in a big plaza near downtown, within walking distance of the parliament building. Inside, the church had only a few overhead heat lamps covering the first few pews. It was, at times, difficult to sit through Mass on a frigid winter day. Even with a hat, gloves, and two pairs of socks, the winter air seeped through the cold stone walls and through all our layers of clothing.

Five-year-old Kyle was thrilled when we arrived at our church back in the States, exclaiming, "I like this church. It's a lot different than our last church. This one has electricity!" Out of the mouths of babes…

St. Catherine's, St. William's, Queen of Peace, St Theresa's, Our Lady of Good Counsel—these parishes hold memories of the sacraments our children received, of the friends we made, and of the faith that grew among us.

At the hotels we stayed in during the months between our moves overseas, the children always jumped right into exploring. They wandered to the pool, down hallway paths to and from our room, roamed outside the hotel and through the lobby, and found the best places to hide—including in the elevator. They learned the fastest route to the dining area, knowing they could run down the hall on their own and get breakfast the minute they woke up.

One year, our Christmas photo was in front of the tree in the hotel lobby of yet another temporary spot in which we were staying. Sometimes I thought it was sad, sometimes funny, but it was our life.

Alexis's preschool teacher that year had the students learn their addresses for a special field trip—they were going to take a school bus to visit each child's home. Every kid proudly stood in front of their door. Alexis stood confidently in front of the hotel for her photoshoot. We couldn't tell if she was sad to be without a real home or proud that she could call the whole hotel her own.

We flew across the Atlantic to get to our new assignment, back to the US to see family, then back across again to start another adventure. To the children, boarding an international flight became routine. The most stressful part of these trips was ensuring that our beloved mixed Lab, Adrienne, was safe in the pressurized cargo area of the plane. Sometimes we'd hear her whining as we sat in our seats, desperate because we were unable to soothe her. Inevitably, one of us would plead with a flight attendant to check on her and report back. Adrienne may not have liked this transatlantic travel, but she dutifully made the trip with us each time. She was tolerant and adapted as quickly, if not more so, than we did at every new location. She was a constant. She was there when we woke up, when we got home from work, and when we went to bed.

As each new Baby Potak arrived, Adrienne would initially tower over them, supervising their activities. As she stayed the same size, though, and each of the children grew, Adrienne would eventually be bumped down another notch in the household pecking order. When the kids were young, she was a great babysitter. She was never frustrated, impatient, or disinterested. The kids adored her—she was one of them. In fact, she was the oldest "sibling."

So, when Adrienne became sick at the age of sixteen and we knew she probably wouldn't make it to our next assignment overseas, it was heartbreaking for us all. Not long before we packed up our household for yet another move, Adrienne developed an unusual growth on her neck. Joe and I panicked. She had never really been sick. We both had a pit in our stomachs. This wasn't normal. Something was wrong. The vet told us the growth was cancerous, but if we had it removed, it was slow-growing enough that she would likely be out of the woods for a while.

Joe and I didn't hesitate. Adrienne underwent surgery, and we felt good about our decision. Within only a few weeks though, the growth came back. We were shattered. Adrienne became so sick that she couldn't eat or walk. We knew it was the end.

We gathered the family and took Adrienne to the vet to say a final goodbye. Joe brought her inside. I couldn't see through my tears. The children and I tried to comfort each other, but it was difficult. The seven of us were so full of sorrow saying goodbye to such a beloved friend and our constant companion. We remained isolated in our grief for a long while.

Chapter Twenty-One

Constant Change

Around the World
1994-2011

For over twenty years, we were like nomads, moving every two or three years. I also gave birth every two or three years until we had five children. This was our life. Constant change.

What if I had taken a different path? Moved only once or twice…or didn't move at all? What if I had a different career…or was a stay-at-home mom? What if I tried to put my career first…or, instead, the family first? What if, somehow, we just really wanted it all?

Things did fall through the cracks. Little things, like not having time to consistently write in my babies' journals, forgetting to pack a school lunch, or falling asleep during the reading of a bedtime story…and a few big things, like forgetting to book plane tickets, missing a doctor's appointment, or losing track of one of the children. Nonetheless, years later, there we were, all together and all intact.

The constant change meant we had to be organized. Details surrounding a move usually fell to me, as the mother and as the employee relocating.

We'd watch as yet another moving company pulled up and loaded all of our possessions into a truck. Moving Joe's Harley-Davidson motorcycle and our Bösendorfer grand piano took special measures. The moving company contracted with an expert in shipping valuable items who built wooden crates for us, on-site, sized specifically to hold the bike and the piano.

We watched as these made-to-order crates and all of our other assorted items, including clothes, books, toys, and pictures, were loaded one box at a time into the cargo bay of the moving van. The truck then traveled to the nearest port, and the containers were loaded onto a ship that crossed the ocean. We periodically heard horror stories of containers lost at sea. Were we ready to lose everything? It was a possibility we had to be prepared for.

On my first assignment overseas, when our household items finally arrived—months after we did—we were giddy, anticipating the pictures for our walls, the next season's clothes, real dishes for the dining table, and playthings for the children. We threw packing paper and cardboard everywhere as we excitedly tore through the boxes.

One by one, we put things away as we found them. I stood next to the kitchen table and bent down to open a box marked "kitchen," glad to finally have pots and pans to make a home-cooked meal. I pulled out the first item wrapped in newspaper. Something was stuck. I wrenched it apart and found a stick of glistening, warm, gooey butter sitting disgustingly in a clear plastic butter dish.

Opening a box marked "bathroom" during a separate move-in, we found a garbage bin still full of wadded-up papers, plastic, and general debris! Not every box held a welcome surprise.

Before every move, we scoured our home, sorted through belongings, and threw out or gave away what we thought we no longer needed—or what was too small, too broken, or too outdated to keep. We pared down our possessions, then placed what was left into piles. We created a pile for things that would stay in the US in a storage unit, a second pile for things that would be sent by ship, knowing it could be months before we saw them again. A third, smaller pile held what we would send by plane. Finally, we made an even smaller pile of things to squeeze into our suitcases—the "absolutely essential" items. There was a whole strategy involved. If it wasn't done right, we'd regret it later.

Despite all the packing, repacking, and discarding, we always had more to get rid of before we could leave. The amount of weight we were allowed to ship was the same whether we were a family of three or a family of seven. It seemed that for every move, even with only the things needed to live with five children, we were shipping more than we were allotted and always had to pay a hefty fee.

Like clockwork, each time we landed in a new city with only a tiny fraction of all we owned, we quickly realized that we didn't really need all the things we had so diligently set aside and claimed were essential. However, much to our chagrin, once our sea shipment did arrive and we were again surrounded by all our "important stuff," the idea of doing without quickly slipped away. Something that was a "nice-to-have" item before, once again, embarrassingly, became a "must-have."

The children entertained themselves at every new place long before their toys and books ever arrived. One of our houses had a stone walkway encircling the perimeter that led to a patio in the back and a two-level terrace in the front. The area was perfect for parties…or playing hide-and-seek. The kids chased each other through the garden, in the front door, and out a side door, down to the basement bedrooms and out the garage. To our horror, as they explored one house on our first day there, it didn't take the boys long to find dozens of dead cockroaches in the water heater room.

Setting up a new home over and over was tedious—the cleaning, the packing, the unpacking, the lost items along the way. The children needed up-to-date immunization records and school forms. We had to find a nanny. We had to find a store to buy the simplest things that we forgot to pack, like nail clippers or extra bibs. We had to find a place to buy fresh milk and diapers. We had to get ourselves out and about and meet the neighbors—again.

We had to find our way around without a car, figure out exchange rates, and find the easiest way to get cash. We had to arrange to vote by absentee ballot. We had to learn how to use the foreign washer and dryer by following directions in a new language. We had to find a new dentist, a new orthodontist, a barbershop, a hairdresser, and a pediatrician.

We had to adjust to new time zones. The more kids we had, the more everyone adapted at different rates. After one long flight from the US, I dropped the family off at our temporary apartment and headed to the office. After six or seven hours, when I was about to collapse, I left work and returned to the hotel to find everyone still fast asleep and sprawled in various positions on the beds.

Joe and I had high expectations for how our children should turn out. We agreed that over the first few years, the schooling and the care they received made a big difference. Over time, we have learned that much more goes into how children turn out than simply the daycare they attend or the games they play as toddlers. Still, we wanted to give them the best start we could. Unfortunately, we often did not have a lot of time to make this ever-so-critical decision. Since we moved so often, leaving sweet, considerate nannies and well-equipped, high-quality daycare facilities behind at every post became traumatic.

Language was sometimes an unfortunate barrier. We needed to be able to understand what had happened all day, what the children ate, what they asked for, what they needed, what they cried about, and what they were happy about. We needed to understand the nanny's schedules, her concerns, and what she needed. Communication, when it came to talking about our kids, was critical.

Habiba, who spoke only Arabic, was our first nanny at our North African post. She was an older woman with an angular face and always had her hair pulled back in a bun. She seemed like a hard worker. We hired Habiba to take care of Kyle during the day for the first several months until he started preschool. She would also keep an eye on Claire when she came home from school, and we planned for her to help take care of Eric once he was born.

Both boys heard Habiba speak Arabic all day. They were content, and life moved along smoothly. But one morning, Habiba didn't arrive. Suddenly, things weren't going according to plan at all. The day started badly, then just kept getting worse. I had a meeting scheduled with an asset. These types of meetings could not easily be changed. Joe was expected at his job at the Embassy. He was working in the Information Management section where the staff was taking advantage of his electrical engineering degree. They needed him early that day to conduct some critical network tests. But we had two small children we couldn't leave alone. *What should we do?*

We waited and waited…and waited. Having the ability to adapt quickly to unexpected changes is critical. It is one of the key tenets of my work. I always try to incorporate it into my daily tasks, but this was different. I had to have a babysitter so I could go off and do that important work. *Why wasn't she here?*

Hours went by. Eventually we realized not only was Habiba not coming that day; she was likely not returning at all. We never did find out why. Maybe she found a better opportunity; maybe the effort to get to our home from her village was too complicated. In the end, it didn't really matter.

We scrambled, juggled schedules, and eventually found Moufida. She was a large, warm, loving lady who smiled all the time. She spoke only a little French and no English, but we made it work. I was able to communicate with her sufficiently in her basic French, and every day Joe used the street-learned Arabic he had mastered by then. Moufida adored Joe for trying, whether she understood what he said or not.

Every day, Moufida lathered Eric's dry skin with olive oil which was her remedy for everything. She regularly prepared delicious local specialties for us—*brik* as an appetizer (a half-circle pastry stuffed with herbs, spinach, or tuna and a runny egg), her signature couscous, and, of course, tajine, a quiche with harissa, olive oil, and dates.

Consistent childcare allowed us to maintain at least a somewhat stable and positive environment for the kids in the midst of all the other changes they were experiencing. We could not risk getting something wrong as we chartered our way forward as parents. But with every move, we faced the same dilemma: who takes off work while we get settled? How do we start our jobs with no daycare in place? Who answers the phone when the school calls?

I could handle more than one or two or three things at once, but when it came to the children and school, I realized I had to listen better. I had to concentrate more. I had to understand that there were priorities that could not be multitasked away. I know there were probably many times we should have been more involved as parents; more involved in decisions regarding classrooms, teachers, what was happening at school, what our kids were doing at school, what they were saying about school, and even what was happening at home when they returned from school.

The children learned how to function in society, how to make decisions for themselves, how to handle things that came up unexpectedly, where to go for answers, and where to go for help. They learned how to gain (and handle the loss of) friends, to influence others and to be influenced wisely, to express themselves clearly and respectfully, and to listen to others. The benefit of learning all of these things convinced us we were making the right decision in choosing this nomadic lifestyle…or at least doing the best we could under the circumstances.

Eleven different schools in seven different cities in five different countries. Every new school meant learning a new routine, new "rules of the road," conferring with new teachers, and understanding a new administration. These moves were difficult for the children. They had it the hardest. They had no say in where we were going to live, what school they would attend, how long we would be there, or where we would go next. We decided it all for them.

As we said goodbye to friends in one neighborhood, a place we had only lived two years, Kyle put his head down in his lap and sobbed. Still in elementary school, he was probably thinking of his friends down the street, or running through the neighbors' backyards, or the sleepovers with his buddies, or the antics at the bus stop and wondering if his days would ever be so fun again.

Remarkably, the children never complained. They would be sad, but they never gave pushback or said they did not want to go. Joe had it tough too. He became entrenched in his jobs, wherever they were. In each of our assignments, Joe worked his contacts and ultimately found interesting, worthwhile, substantive positions. Some were on the local economy, like his job with Booz Allen Hamilton in Paris. Some were positions at the US Embassy in the country where we were assigned. Every time, though, he made friends and worked hard. He was dedicated and loyal. But then, he would have to leave again.

Chapter Twenty-Two

Back in America

New York
2003-2005

Right after Katrina was born in the summer of 2003, we took a two-year assignment back in the US. We weren't in the most exotic of places, but where we landed wasn't really up to me and at least we were all together.

I was initially assigned to New York City. It would have been fun, exciting, something new and different. I love cities. However, with a big family, life in Manhattan—where I would have been required to live—would have been complicated and tough financially. Our expenses would far exceed our income. How would we afford groceries and transportation for a family of seven? How would we pay for schools for five children? How would we find enough green space to throw the ball and play outside?

I went to New York on a house-hunting trip. I returned worried, disappointed, and very disheartened. Yet, I was willing to try to make it work. I felt it was my duty.

As if to prove to me that we were never really in control in the first place, I was given the opportunity to move to

Upstate New York instead—to establish and build a new office and, at the same time, take advantage of a much easier standard of living.

An exhilarating, dynamic, city life with all kinds of entertainment, museums, restaurants, and people, or a calmer, more suburban life with lots of green space and cheaper prices? Intense, nonstop hours working on critical issues or an opportunity to create something new from the ground up?

We chose the suburbs. It felt like the right choice.

In this new position, I worked closely with the FBI. Together, we built up a repository of information about potential threats, terrorist plots, and people supporting terrorist activities. We shared information and collaborated on contacts and sources. I explained the CIA's mission to my FBI colleagues, all the while at home making sure my family was adapting to their new city, their new home, their new schools, and their new friends.

I was part of the Joint Terrorism Task Force (JTTF), an effort established after 9/11 to share information about terrorist threats. It was made up of not only the CIA and the FBI but also officers from the Drug Enforcement Agency, Naval Intelligence, Secret Service, the Bureau of Alcohol, Tobacco, Firearms and Explosives, US Immigration and Customs Enforcement, US Postal Inspection Service, Federal Air Marshal Service, US Diplomatic Security Service, US Army Criminal Investigation Command, US Customs and Border Patrol, and local law enforcement organizations.

This assignment was unique. I would not be spending days meeting recruited agents who had secrets about the plans and intentions of foreign governments. I would not be sneaking around corners at night. I would not be driving long surveillance detection routes in order to determine if someone was following me. Rather, I was asked to create a new and positive relationship between my office and the FBI. Unfortunately, it became a daunting mission. The special agent in charge (SAC) of this particular FBI office was not a fan of the CIA. He really had no use for us, and he told me that quite bluntly. Nonetheless, I had to slowly and methodically demonstrate to him that we could help with his cases and that I was not there to take any credit away from the Bureau or his agents. I needed to prove to him that I could, in fact, assist them in ways he might not have realized.

I relished the challenge, but I was also under pressure by my headquarters to produce results—primarily in the form of reports, but also new contacts who could be useful when seeking information about domestic terrorist plots. My responsibilities did not coincide the way I had envisioned they might. Every day was a challenge. Every week I had to send into my headquarters numbers far below what they expected. Yet, I knew I was making great progress with my JTTF colleagues and, more importantly, with the SAC in whose building I was borrowing space. I had an excellent rapport built with the law enforcement officers who went out on calls and with the FBI agents who introduced me to their cases. But, in the end, that didn't matter as much as the number of reports I wasn't producing.

It was a difficult year of work. For every step forward, I felt I was taking two steps back in my career.

New York City was only about three hours away by train, making it an easy day trip when I needed to visit the head office. It was a hot day in the middle of August when I travelled to Manhattan for a midmorning briefing followed by a working lunch. I finished my meetings in midtown by three in the afternoon, stopped at a corner deli for a bottle of water, and then hailed a taxi for the short ride back to Penn Station five blocks away. I was on schedule to catch a late afternoon train home, which would get me there in time to read a bedtime story to my babies.

In the cab, I took advantage of a few minutes of downtime and started to daydream. I looked out the window at the city. I loved all the motion, the noise, the colors, the changing scenes. My mind drifted to wondering what it would have been like to live and work here every day.

Then, after only a few minutes, I noticed something different, something odd happening up ahead. It seemed cars were stopped for no reason. Then I saw that the traffic lights were out. People started drifting out of the shops and milling around on the sidewalks. My cab was only inching forward. I was going to miss my train.

Exasperated, I threw some cash in the direction of the driver, grabbed my briefcase, and stepped out of the taxi. Jostling past people who seemed to be just standing with no purpose except to keep me from moving forward, I hustled along the remaining few blocks to Penn Station. As I approached the entrance, people were streaming out and coming in my direction. No one was going in. Above the commotion, I heard people yelling that the station was being evacuated. *Evacuated? What was going on?* This was all so out of the ordinary. Things were supposed to run smoothly, especially in a busy city like New York. Trains ran on time. People kept moving ahead.

It must be a mistake. I quickly turned and walked in the opposite direction to the Port Authority bus station. I knew the city well enough to know this was the easiest and simplest alternative to get back home. But, as I walked the eight short blocks, people continued to fill the sidewalks and the streets, and I couldn't make any sense of what was happening.

Due to a major power outage, New York City had gone dark, along with most of the Northeast region of the US. On that swelteringly hot day in 2003, there were no trains, no buses, and no electricity, so no air-conditioning, no power, and no lights. It was a massive blackout.

Port Authority had also been evacuated. I turned around and walked back to Penn Station, hoping to be first in line to get the next train heading north once the power did return. I was certain things would improve within the hour. Darkness began engulfing the terminal. People were frantically trying to find a way home. Hours multiplied. I realized that neither I, nor anyone else, was going anywhere anytime soon.

Things did not improve. I resigned myself to staying put until the power was restored. I found a small, bare, concrete square of floor on the main shopping level of Penn Station, the escalators leading down to the train tracks all silenced. I was surrounded by hundreds of other stranded travelers trying to find their own space. I settled in. My briefcase was under my head for a bit of padding, and so I could keep it safe. My shoes were off to ease my sweaty, sore feet, and I held onto the one water bottle I was able to find. I eventually fell into a very fitful sleep.

A place where people were usually completely immersed in their own thoughts as they moved fast to catch trains or make meetings now, in this time of crisis, became one giant community. Everyone was sharing what they could—phone chargers, water bottles, personal stories, and even space on the cement floor.

As for me, I had been on a mission…and now, for the first time in a long time, I wasn't. I couldn't go anywhere. No one could.

So, I took advantage of *time*. Lying there, trying to drift off to sleep on the cold, hard, dirty train station floor, I was aware of the fact that I was surrounded by strangers instead of my family and friends. There was absolutely nothing I could do. My mind began to drift. I looked back on my life, reminiscing.

Hours later, as it became light, I awoke. I struggled to a standing position, then followed people venturing outside to see the sun. On the corner was the very welcome scene of Red Cross booths offering granola bars and cups of hot, freshly brewed coffee to us stranded travelers.

I made it home that evening. I was among the lucky ones. I was thankful that I had only to worry about myself throughout that whole ordeal. My children had been safe and sound asleep in their own beds.

Chapter Twenty-Three

A Different Kind of Mom

Around the World
1996-2013

Another transatlantic move. We were back in the US. After unexpectedly leaving Paris in the mid-1990s, and despite the sudden change of direction we had to abruptly endure, our life seemed rather idyllic. Our jobs were not too far from our house, and neither of us had very stressful positions. Joe and I were both home every evening. We socialized with neighbors. Claire and Kyle had settled in well at their preschools. It seemed quite…perfect. Why would I ever want to change things? Why would I give up such a calm, conventional, predictable life? For the first time since I began my career, I thought very seriously about leaving it for something more stable, something more ordinary.

I started applying to jobs in the area. I interviewed for a local government position, an economic analyst job with the Public Utilities Commission (PUC). I was still on maternity leave, so on the day of the interview, I had plenty of time to get ready. Searching through my closet, I found a knee-length, sleeveless black dress that looked professional and smart. I printed out several copies of my newly updated resume and wrote down some notes to myself about the PUC, along with comments about how I would convince them that they could benefit from someone with my background. I drank a tall glass of refreshing iced tea, then drove the ten minutes to the PUC offices.

An hour later, I was sitting in front of a panel of three people watching as they passed around copies of my resume. The stern looking individuals began with a few general questions.

"Tell us about your work in Paris."

"Can you describe the senior-level briefings you had to prepare?"

"Please elaborate on the impact that the reports you wrote had."

After only a few minutes, though, the questions changed focus. They became less about the work I was doing and more about why I was doing the work.

"How did you get this job with the State Department?"

"How were you able to travel to all those incredible places?"

The interview seemed to be going in a totally different direction than I had anticipated. I quickly realized my interviewers were asking questions now because they were intrigued about the job that I was *currently* doing. Were they envious? What were they trying to find out? Was the job with the PUC even a real job? My spy brain started to whirl.

As the questioning continued, I began to think that maybe I didn't really want to work for the PUC. I started to believe that I may already have the perfect job. I just had to continue to make it work with a family. It was an epiphany that stayed with me and bolstered me over the years when the going got tough. The grass was already pretty green on my side.

Throughout my career, I had to travel regularly, often out of the country. I called home as frequently as I could when I was away, but struggled with being so far from the family. Talking to the children over the phone was stressful. They never seemed interested in staying on a call for very long, telling me about their day, or answering my questions. Maybe it was difficult because I wasn't standing right in front of them.

Kyle frequently had his mouth pressed up so tight against the phone, jabbering about something he was excited about without even stopping to take a breath. Or, there'd be long periods of silence where I thought he might have put the phone down to go get a snack and then forgot we were even talking. Once, when I told him I was getting on an airplane to reassure him I'd be home soon, he didn't seem excited. Instead, he just asked, "But, Mommy, how are you going to get down from the airplane? Maybe you can get a rope and just climb down," he so kindly suggested. I did miss being next to him at that moment watching his face as he tried to figure it all out.

If I was going to succeed in this life I chose, I knew I had to put aside my worries, my hesitation, and my constant anxiousness about the kids being at home and without me. It wasn't easy. I should have been able to get used to it, but I never seemed to relax.

After Claire was born, all I wanted to do was sit and stare at her. Once back at work, all I thought about was how I missed twirling around the living room with her, singing to her, just the two of us.

As my return to work got closer after each birth, I grew more anxious. Joe came home from his office and often found me not far from the same spot I had been in when he left earlier that morning.

"I am trying to wean her," I lamented, "but there are too many bottles, too many steps. Claire was hungry. It's too complicated," I protested, "and so I gave up." Then I finally admitted to myself and to Joe, "It was just too easy to sit down and nurse her like I had been doing all along."

Joe responded with a sympathetic look, then began boiling bottles and setting them aside for me to try again the next day.

Back at work, I sorely missed taking the children to the park any day I wanted. I missed comforting Kyle when he accidentally stepped on a fire ant hill. I missed pushing Eric on the swing in the mornings. I missed taking Alexis to school. I missed watching all the changes in the children when they were small.

After Katrina was born, I knew she would probably be our last, and I panicked. I worried that I would forget all those moments when they smelled so sweet and fit so easily into my arms. I was unhappy thinking those moments might all be behind me…forever.

I tried to convince myself, over and over, that the children would be fine. I told myself that I had important work to do in the office. I knew, somewhere deep down in my soul, the sadness of leaving my newborn would pass. Still, it took a long time before I stopped asking myself if my baby missed me or if she wondered where I had gone all day.

The back-and-forth pull of emotions between thinking I needed to be at work and knowing I needed to be with the children wore me down. I knew I was doing something important, and while no one was indispensable, I had responsibilities to others that I needed to fulfill.

Nonetheless, once back in the office and following a daily routine, I always felt good about my decision to return.

I realized how grateful I needed to be for the opportunities my profession was providing all of us.

Breaking cover was always a very big deal. Even telling a member of my own family what I actually did for a living was never something to take lightly. Claire learned what I did long before the others. I explained my job in general terms to her as soon as I knew she was mature enough to understand. I told Kyle a few years later. The other three only learned the real story at the end of my career when they attended my retirement ceremony at CIA headquarters. Eric's only comment about the "cool place" I worked was, "How come Kyle got to know about it before me?"

There was always so much pressure to do things right. There was pressure to recruit good agents, to not get caught, to teach young officers the right way to work our craft, and to teach them to stay honest to our ethical code. There was pressure to be a good mother, to ensure the children ate healthy, to give them opportunities, to keep them safe, to teach them to be kind, and to help them understand the world. There was so much to do. There was so much to remember. *How could I do it all?* I asked myself this question countless times.

I seemed to always be planning for something. Planning what to make for family dinners, planning how to make time for Claire's music recital, planning Kyle's birthday party, planning what snacks to pack for Eric's T-ball game, planning who was going to be home to put the children to bed, and planning our next trip back to the US so we could stay in touch with family.

I planned meetings with my agents and planned for alternatives in case the first plan hit a bump. I planned when I would meet certain people for lunch or dinner. I planned which information to write up first. I made lists. I rewrote the lists. Important things I had to remember for work I kept in my head and hoped I wouldn't forget.

The pressure of the job grew as my role in the organization evolved into management. Not only did I have to continue to look for and collect intelligence and keep my agents safe, I also had to ensure I was properly mentoring the junior officers. I had to teach them the right way to do things, making sure they understood the importance of the job and that they took what they were doing seriously. I had to provide them with suggestions on how to balance a demanding job with a satisfying personal life. It was incumbent upon me, as someone with more experience in the field, to demonstrate how rewarding and satisfying the career of an operations officer could be. I felt strongly that if the young officers saw how exciting and important our career was, they would naturally excel at it.

Both as an operations officer and as a mother, I often held high expectations for those around me. As I learned the trade and better understood the most efficient ways to obtain information, and as I saw the need sometimes to hustle to get the answers, I would find myself encouraging my subordinates to pick up the pace.

This was not always met with the best results. Though it took time, I eventually learned that I could not force my expectations on others—even those whose careers I was responsible for guiding. In hindsight, I should have spent less time telling others to hustle and more time just doing it so they could see me as an example.

Part of my efforts in encouraging people around me to move faster, to work harder, and to do more was simply because I felt there was no time to waste.

Being a manager, specifically a manager in the CIA where the job was to mentor and guide officers in such a unique career, was difficult. It meant helping them put aside their preconceived notions of how things were done and instilling a sense of importance and pride in the work we did every day.

My life as a mom and my life as a CIA officer collided over and over. I was pregnant during almost every assignment. I was always walking, working, shopping, and mothering. Since no one ever expected a pregnant woman to be a spy, I could go anywhere and meet anyone and rarely arouse suspicion. No one ever thought I was anything but just a mom. I attended diplomatic receptions, waddling around the room with my glass of water, and introduced myself to those I felt were of interest to talk to and those I wanted to learn more about. I was often the most non-threatening person at the function.

I was eight months pregnant with Alexis when I had a meeting with an agent across Europe, hundreds of kilometers away. We saw each other every two months and I was getting really good information from him. I used an alias to travel to and conduct these meetings. All logistics—from the moment I left my home to the moment I arrived at the meeting site and then returned home again—had to be perfectly planned and executed. I did this often. I knew what I had to do.

In this case, though, the long train ride portion of the trip was difficult. I was uncomfortable, tired, hungry, and, with every minute that passed, worried I might go into labor.

Memories rushed into my head…and my heart. I recalled my water breaking as I hurried through the airport to meet my CIA colleague years before. I remembered another time being panicked as my contractions became stronger while I tried to let my daughter finish her playdate at the pool. Now, I wondered if I was risking my baby's health by being so immersed in a job I had to finish. I wasn't near a hospital, I wasn't near a doctor, I wasn't near Joe, and I was using a different name once again. Allowing myself a moment of anxiety, I asked myself how long I could keep this up, this life of being everything—a wife, mother, and spy all at once.

I was worried about the meeting. What if, when I finally did arrive, the street was blocked, closed, or somehow inaccessible? What if my agent wasn't at the location as planned? What if my documents didn't withstand scrutiny? What if I got hurt? What if I went into labor—with a name that wasn't really mine? What if I couldn't meet my agent because I was giving birth instead?

I was on a train heading west. I clutched my fake documents in my hand. The conductor came through the car and stopped at my seat. "Ticket and passport, please," he said gruffly in the local language. I smiled up at him, outwardly confident but trembling inside, and handed over my documents. He glanced at them and then, without hesitating, continued down the train car. I knew my documents were solid, but situations like this still made my heart stop. So much to think about. So much to plan for. So much to do.

Afterword

Sometimes I think of my life as very normal—husband, kids, work, home, business trips, family dinners, school projects, mentoring subordinates at the office, sporting events, entertaining friends, church on Sundays, parent-teacher conferences.

As I look back on it all, I realize that it has not been so ordinary. In fact, my life has been quite extraordinary. The experiences we have had as a family, the places we have gone, the things we have seen and learned, the friends we have made, and even the pain we have experienced together all seem very far from ordinary.

When I contemplate why and how it all began, I realize my career path actually came about because of the way I was raised, the tools and opportunities I was given by my parents, and the lessons I learned from them.

There are now many women working in the CIA. However, there are still very few women who choose a life as a clandestine operations officer while at the same time raising a large family. During my career, I had to think differently than others. I had to surround myself with people who understood what I needed and where I was going. I had to rely on my husband, on my instincts, and on God more than ever.

I want to tell my story so women starting out in their careers will realize that with some grit, determination, patience, and a little bit of luck, they can have a very fulfilling professional *and* personal life—at the same time, no matter what career they choose. Even if they choose to be a CIA operations officer.

I want to describe the lessons I learned, the opportunities I had, and the struggles I saw in working and raising a family. Hopefully, readers of this book can take the good, eliminate the unnecessary, and pass on the important parts to others around them.

I want to tell my story so my children will always remember to be grateful for both the opportunities they have had and the struggles they have endured.

I want to tell this story for myself—so I can finally realize that it *was* all worth it.